3o~minute sewing

3o~minute sewing

what can you sew in half an hour or less?

heather m. love

BARRON'S

A QUINTET BOOK

First edition for North America and the Philippines
published in 2014 by Barron's Educational Series, Inc.

All inquiries should be addressed to:
Barron's Educational Series, Inc.
250 Wireless Boulevard
Hauppauge, NY 11788
www.barronseduc.com

Library of Congress Control Number: 2014931542

ISBN: 978-1-4380-0410-5

QTT.TMS

This book was designed and produced by
Quintet Publishing Limited
4th Floor, Sheridan House,
114-116 Western Road,
Hove, BN3 1DD, UK

Project Editor: Caroline Elliker
Designer: Anna Gatt
Diagrams: Gareth Butterworth
Photographer: Sussie Bell
Art Director: Michael Charles
Managing Editor: Emma Bastow
Publisher: Mark Searle

Printed in China by 1010 Printing Group Limited

9 8 7 6 5 4 3 2 1

 contents

introduction

Not a minute to spare? The patterns in this book are designed to get you sewing quickly and easily with simple projects that can be completed in 30-minute sessions. Whether you are an absolute beginner or an experienced stitcher, you'll lose no time finding the patterns best suited to your ability.

Basic (see pages 10–37): With a few fun projects, beginners will see just how simple sewing can be. There's no need to be intimidated, just take things step-by-step. The projects in this chapter are designed to be stress-free. No matter what your level, there's always something new to learn, so jump right in.

Intermediate (see pages 38–67): Now that you know the basics, this chapter will help you take your skills to the next level. Garments, gifts, and home décor, the projects in this section will inspire creative solutions to common dilemmas and have you stitching like a DIY diva. Remember: Practice makes perfect.

Savvy (see pages 68–99): The sky's the limit—there's nothing you can't do. Strut your stuff and continue to develop your abilities with new techniques and challenges. This chapter encourages you to try something new with each project and grow your sewing skills beyond your wildest dreams.

Essential Equipment (page 100), Working with Fabric (page 104), and **Techniques and Skill Builders (page 108):** All include useful information to ensure a successful sewing experience. You'll learn the basics of pattern layout and cutting, commonly used finishing and hand-sewing techniques, proper use and maintenance of sewing equipment, and troubleshooting procedures. At the back of the book there are also several project templates (page 116).

TIPS FOR FASTER RESULTS

· Read pattern instructions from start to finish before you begin to work on your project. This will inform you about the process and prevent unnecessary surprises.

· Gather all materials and equipment before you begin so time isn't wasted looking for the tools you need.

· Relax and enjoy—rushing can cause unnecessary stress, which leads to mistakes.

SPECIAL NOTES

Where seam allowance is unspecified, projects should be made up using a ¼-in (6-mm) seam allowance. The assembly of all projects is achievable in the 30-minute time allotment, but preparation is not included in project times. Depending on your sewing abilities and familiarity with techniques, some projects may take a bit longer for some individuals. If you are new to sewing, do not be discouraged. With a little practice your project completion times will be reduced greatly.

30~minute projects

basic

bike streamers
page 11

kite
page 12

crown of flowers
page 15

gift bags
page 16

gift tags
page 17

cloth dog flyer
page 18

dog leash
page 19

jar label wraps
page 20

infinity towel
page 21

tea towel
page 22

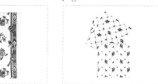

recycled throw
page 23

matchbook sewing kit *page 24*

curtains
page 27

baby burp cloth
page 28

ribbon wristlet
page 29

shrug
page 30

apron
page 33

hair accessories
page 34

hair band
page 35

obi belt
page 36

intermediate

stuffed owls
page 39

cat tent
page 40

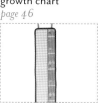

juggling balls
page 41

tic-tac-toe
page 42

crayon caddy
page 44

door sign
page 45

growth chart
page 46

bleacher seat
page 48

picnic blanket
page 49

throw pillows
page 51

eye mask
page 52

pincushion
page 54

wall pockets
page 55

glasses case
page 56

tote bag
page 58

reversible clutch
page 59

halter top
page 60

wrap skirt
page 62

shower cap
page 65

hand warmers
page 66

savvy

finger puppets
page 69

flat doll dress up
page 70

stuffed bunny
page 72

robot rattle
page 74

stroller cozy
page 75

paper plane mobile
page 76

fingerless gloves
page 78

silhouette applique
page 79

tailor's ham and
sleeve roll *page 80*

change purse
page 81

phone wallet
page 82

lunch sack
page 84

casserole carrier
page 85

bike basket
page 87

book cover
page 88

kimono blouse
page 90

men's tie
page 92

weekend bag
page 95

slippers
page 96

superhero cape
and cuffs *page 99*

bike streamers

Remember jumping on your bike and riding down to the corner store to buy penny candy with a saved coin or two? With the wind in your hair, the streamers on your handlebars screamed with excitement, and you blew by the other kids in the neighborhood. Freedom found, surely you were the luckiest kid in the world...

MATERIALS

¼ yd (¼ m) medium-weight to heavyweight cotton

¼ yd (¼ m) batting

6–18 yds (6–18 m) ribbon

Thread to match fabric

½-in (1.25-cm) wide Velcro

EQUIPMENT

Quilter's square

Fabric scissors

Disappearing ink marker

PREPARATION

With your quilter's square, measure and mark out two batting and four fabric panels to 6 x 7 in (15 x 17.5 cm). Cut out.

ASSEMBLY

Align two of your fabric panels with right sides facing, then place one of the batting panels on top. Pin the layers together and stitch three sides closed with a ½-in (1.25-cm) seam allowance, leaving one of the 7-in (17.5-cm) sides open. Clip the corners. Reach between the fabric layers and turn the work right side out. Fold the unfinished edges over by ½ in (1.25 cm) and insert into the opening. Press seams.

Cut ribbons to your desired size—for best results choose a length between 12–18 in (30–45 cm). Fold ribbon lengths in half and pin the folded edges into place along the inside edge of the open end. Topstitch opening closed.

Repeat process to make a second streamer. To finish, attach Velcro to each of the 6-in (15-cm) sides so that the hook and loop are matched at the overlap edge.

HELPFUL HINT

Leftover and scrap ribbons are great for this project. Remember shorter and wider ribbons will use up less yardage.

projects

kite

When gentle winds begin to blow, it's time to head to greener pastures for a bit of high flying fun. This basic kite model offers a wonderful opportunity to introduce kids to the lighter side of math and science. Spark their creativity and inspire a lifetime of learning.

PREPARATION

Lay the ripstop nylon on a flat surface and cut out a rectangle 30 x 40 in (75 x 100 cm). Using the disappearing ink marker and ruler, and referring to fig. 1, mark the center of each short side 15 in (37.5 cm) from the edge—connect these points to mark a center line 40 in (100 cm) long (line A/B). Measure 10 in (25 cm) from top edge and draw a line perpendicular to the first across the fabric (line C/D). Mark a line between points A and D, and between points A and C. Referring to fig. 2, mark a line between points B and C and points B and D. Trim fabric away ½ in (1.25 cm) outside of the marked lines for seam allowance.

For added reinforcement cut four 2 x 2 in (5 x 5 cm) squares from your fabric. Fold each square diagonally across and stitch ¼ in (6 mm) from folded edge. Now place each of these triangles at points A, B, C, and D, with the hypotenuse (folded side) toward the center of the kite body and catheti (angled sides) aligned to marked edges centering the middle point in each corner; pin in place.

Cut ⅜-in (1-cm) diameter dowels to fit between points C–D (29 in/72.5 cm) and A–B (39 in/97.5 cm). Check these measurements before cutting as you may have slight differences if your seam allowance or stitching varies.

ASSEMBLY

Fold seam allowance over twice by ¼ in (6 mm) each, pin in place, and stitch along marked line. Stitch two parallel seams ½ in (1.25 cm) apart at center of each triangle perpendicular to the hypotenuse. The dowel should fit snugly into this slot. Install ¼-in (6-mm) grommets 1 in (2.5 cm) from the center point on each side of center line.

For kite tail, layer and fold ribbons in half, and attach to bottom (point B).

Insert the dowels into the pockets so that they cross at the center point. You will need to flex these slightly when inserting into the reinforcing tabs at the corners. Tie kite string to the 6-in (15-cm) dowel handle and wrap the length around it. Tie the other end of the kite string through the grommets and around the crossed dowels so that it is firmly attached. Go fly a kite!

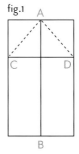

fig.1

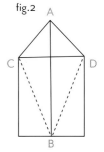

fig.2

fig.3

crown of flowers

Conjure up the magic of woodland elves, indulge your inner fairy, or add a feminine, bohemian vibe to any wedding party with this enchanting hair accessory. This charming garland will beautifully adorn your tresses for special occasions or anytime you want to feel pretty.

PREPARATION

With a measuring tape, determine head size so that you can estimate the garland length. You will want to make a garland that is a bit smaller than your actual head measurement, so that you can tie it firmly at the back with the ribbons.

Scan and print or photocopy the leaf and flower templates onto paper and cut out with craft scissors. Lay out leaf templates in a staggered fashion on either side of a sheet of green felt and trace outlines using a disappearing ink marker. Connect the leaf shapes on opposite sides with two parallel lines to create stem outlines. Cut out 25–35 stems in a variety of lengths. With flower templates, trace and cut out 30–40 blossoms from desired colors.

Overlap and twist stem lengths together to create a bundle of desired fullness that is just shorter than your head measurement. String flower shapes onto several lengths of green thread and wrap these threads around the stem bundle several times to firmly secure. Pull flowers and leaves to the outside of the bundle and arrange bulk evenly.

ASSEMBLY

Use running stitch to secure layers together and gather for some fullness. Layer two or three ribbons to create a band and place flower bundles at center. Knot ribbons together on either side of the bundle. With embroidery thread, attach flower bundle to ribbons with long, even running stitches that penetrate the ribbon layers. Tie crown into place with a bow and trim ribbons to desired length.

SEE TEMPLATES ON PAGE 116

MATERIALS

An assortment of felt sheets: Shades of green for stems and leaves, and white for flowers

Green sewing thread

2 yds (2 m) each of several ribbons in colors to complement flowers

Embroidery thread

EQUIPMENT

Measuring tape

Disappearing ink marker

Craft and fabric scissors

Hand-sewing needle

HELPFUL HINT

Feeling adventurous? Look to your garden or a local park for seasonal inspiration. Sketch your favorite flora and render your unique interpretation in felt to celebrate the season.

gift bags

Everybody loves a party, and these simple stitched goodie bags will make your next bash a smashing success without breaking the bank or ruining the planet. Send guests home with a booty bag that can be used to stow treasures again and again.

PREPARATION

Measure and mark out a panel 6½ x 11 in (16.25 x 27.5 cm) onto your fabric, then cut out.

ASSEMBLY

With wrong sides facing, fold fabric in half so that the shorter edges meet at the top. Stitch the side seams together with a ¼-in (6-mm) seam allowance. Fold length of ribbon in half and pin it to one seam 2 in (5 cm) below the unfinished edge at the top of the bag. (At this point, you may want to pin the excess ribbon at the center to ensure that only the folded section is stitched into the seam.) Trim bottom corners, turn work inside out and press seams flat. Stitch along side seams again, this time using a ½-in (1.25-cm) seam allowance.

Finish the top edge of the bag with a 1-in (2.5-cm) double fold hem (see page 111). Turn bag right side out and press seams.

HELPFUL HINT

Fabric with a width of 44 in (110 cm) will make six 5 x 7 in (12.5 x 17.5 cm) gift bags. Experiment with handles, embellishments and closures for variety and fun. This simple, flat bag is generally best for smaller items, but you can make a larger version to fit a particular gift. To do this, carefully measure the item you would like to wrap and modify the pattern according to your measurements. Give thoughtful consideration to the depth of your item and compensate for this along the height and width of your bag as needed to be sure items fit into the finished sack.

gift tags

Create a quick gift, send a smile or leave a happy little note for your dearest. This project relies on a bit of improvisation to cleverly combine bits of discarded paper, fabric, and trim. So raid your recycling bin and ransack those bags of unused sewing scraps to artfully "remake" cards, gift tags, journals, and more.

PREPARATION

Begin by laying out scraps, strips or squares of fabric so they overlap in a pleasing manner. Have fun with this process, mixing and matching colors to suit your mood. As you work, use your rotary cutter and a mat to trim pieces and remove unsightly strands or even out edges. Your layout should be slightly larger than the area you are trying to cover so that you can trim away the excess for a perfectly fitted collage.

ASSEMBLY

Stitch fabric and trimmings to cardstock in the configured layout. Play with zigzag, decorative stitches, or geometric lines to accentuate pattern choices or other elements of your collage layout. Be sure to backstitch a few stitches at the beginning and end of each line of stitches to keep them from unraveling.

Trim away excess overlap and gently remove stray threads. Allow some of the roughness to remain in your collaged pieces—this adds to the personality and lends a unique, artful quality.

MATERIALS

Fabric scraps

Thread to match project

Cardstock

Ribbon, grommets, buttons or other trimmings (optional)

EQUIPMENT

Quilter's square

Rotary cutter and mat

Craft and fabric scissors

Heavy-duty sewing machine needle

HELPFUL HINT

You should use a heavyweight needle for this process. Remember that needles used with paper will dull faster than those used with fabric, so change them often to prevent breakage and be sure to discard after use.

cloth dog flyer

Kids and pups alike will love this amazing fabric flyer. Stitch one up in a bright, fun fabric and watch it fly. Pack and go for hours of entertainment at the beach, in the park, or on a campout.

PREPARATION

Fold fabric with wrong sides facing. With tailor's chalk or disappearing ink marker, place saucer (for small flyer) or dinner plate (for large flyer) face down on fabric and trace shape. Cut out tracing.

ASSEMBLY

With right sides facing and raw edges aligned, attach wider side of bias around the edge of disc. Seam ends of bias together at a 45-degree angle. (See Baby Burp Cloth, page 28, for more advice on how to apply double fold bias tape, and page 108, for basics.)

Trim cord to appropriate length and insert into bias pocket. Fold bias over and topstitch around edging.

HELPFUL HINT

Be warned, the disc will not fly properly without the additional weight of the piping cord at the edges, so don't skip this important step. No piping cord on hand? Use a bit of laundry line instead.

MATERIALS

¼ –⅓ yd (¼–⅓ m) medium-weight to heavyweight canvas fabric

⅔–⅞ yd (⅔–⅞ m) double fold bias tape and matching piping cord

EQUIPMENT

Tailor's chalk or disappearing ink marker

Saucer or dinner plate

Fabric scissors

dog leash

Collars are optional with this trendsetting slip-on lead. With no fussy buckles or clips, just gently slip it over your dog's head and position it high on the neck for a comfortable and controlled stroll. Personalize it with a bit of ribbon and you're ready for a walk on the wild side.

PREPARATION

Pin decorative ribbon along center of webbing and topstitch it into place along either edge.

ASSEMBLY

To make handle, fold one end over by 6 in (15 cm) with ribbon side out, and tuck a 1-in (2.5-cm) section back under this fold. Stitch through all three layers at the fold and through two layers just above the folded-under edge, to enclose cut edge. Reinforce seams with an "X" if desired.

With ribbon side facing out, slip the other end of the webbing through the D ring. Fold over 2 in (5 cm) and topstitch a seam next to the D ring. Fold remaining edge back under and stitch through all three layers to enclose rough edges. Reinforce seams if desired.

Slip a length of leash through the D ring to create a collar loop, then slip this over your dog's head.

MATERIALS

2 yds (2 m) ¾-in (2-cm) wide decorative ribbon

2 yds (2 m) 1-in (2.5-cm) wide cotton or nylon webbing

D ring to match webbing width

Heavy-duty thread to match ribbon/webbing

EQUIPMENT

Straight pins

Fabric scissors

Heavy-duty sewing machine needle

jar label wraps

Mason jars are the star of your DIY holiday season with these adorable linen note keepers. Canning, pickling or just jamming out in the kitchen, these wraps will dress up any jar and deliver a jolly message to recipients, along with your tasty treats.

PREPARATION

Cut the embroidery cloth into three 12-in (30-cm) pieces. Take each piece and fold bottom edge up by 3 in (7.5 cm); pin and press. Cut ribbon into three 27-in (68.5-cm) and six 5½-in (13.75-cm) sections.

ASSEMBLY

Pin and stitch the shorter sections of ribbon along the unfinished edges of the embroidery cloth pieces leaving ½-in (1.25-cm) excess at the top and bottom edges (fig. 1). Fold attached ribbon to the back of the work and tuck the unfinished edges under at the top and bottom to finish edges. Fold a 27-in (68.5-cm) section of ribbon in half and slip it into place under the finishing ribbon along one side so that it is centered (fig. 2). Pin layers together and edge-stitch the ribbon into place. Repeat the ribbon finishing along the other edge, this time excluding the longer ribbon at the center.

Place wrap around jar like an apron and tie the ribbon with a bow at the front. Include a thank you note, recipe card or other warm wishes in the folded pocket at the front for an added smile.

MATERIALS

To make three wraps:

1 yd (1 m) 7½-in (19-cm) wide linen embroidery cloth

3¼ yd (3¼ m) chevron ribbon or twill tape

Thread to match ribbon/cloth

EQUIPMENT

Yardstick or quilter's square

Fabric scissors or rotary cutter and mat

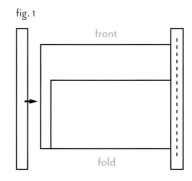

fig. 1

front

fold

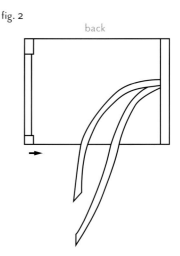

fig. 2

back

infinity towel

These towels were inspired by a beautiful vintage pair given to me by a dear friend when I moved into a new apartment. She loves vintage as much as I do and I think of her every time I see them looped over my wooden towel rack in the kitchen. Made more beautiful with a length of vintage cloth, they are infinitely useful.

MATERIALS

2½ yds (2½ m) 18-in (45-cm) wide linen toweling

Thread to match fabric

EQUIPMENT

Fabric scissors

PREPARATION

Cut linen toweling in half so that you have two panels measuring 18 in (45 cm) x 1¼ yds (1¼ m). Fold each piece in half with wrong sides facing.

ASSEMBLY

Working on each piece in turn, stitch cut edges together ¼ in (6 mm) from raw edge, stitching along this edge only. Trim seam allowance to ⅛ in (3 mm) and turn work so right sides are facing. Press seam flat and stitch along edge again ½ in (1.25 cm) from the first seam to enclose raw edges in a French seam (see page 112).

Press edge, turn towel right side out and hang.

tea towel

Few things are as indispensable in the kitchen as this everyday essential. More than a dish towel, this potholder, plate wiper, and pressing cloth in one should always be close at hand whether it's your turn to cook or clean-up.

PREPARATION

Begin by cutting your fabric to size. Cut a ½-yd (½-m) piece of fabric into two equal pieces by halving it along the bolt fold.

ASSEMBLY

Kitchen towels are a great way to practice your hemming skills. If you are new to hemming, you may want to review the double fold hem tutorial on page 111 before starting this project.

Take one of your fabric pieces and fold the first edge over twice, pinning along the fold closest to the center. Topstitch along the edge of this first fold. Continue to work around the panel clockwise, repeating this process of folding and pinning for each side in sequence as you move from one edge of the panel to the next. On the fourth side, fold a 3-in (7.5-cm) section of twill tape in half and insert the cut edges under the hem fold before pinning. Topstitch final edge and hang towel from loop.

Repeat process to make a second towel.

MATERIALS

½ yd (½ m) medium-weight to heavyweight linen or cotton

6 in (15 cm) ½-in (1.25-cm) wide twill tape or ribbon

Thread to match fabric

EQUIPMENT

Quilter's square

Rotary cutter and mat

Straight pins

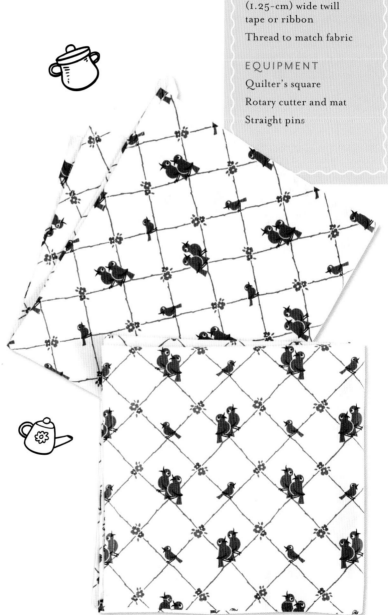

recycled throw

Shabby, moth-eaten sweaters are perfectly repurposed to create this beautiful felted throw. This last-minute gift is sure to make a big impression at your next housewarming party, and will impress without breaking the bank.

PREPARATION

Cut felt into 24 rectangles each measuring 5 in x 11 in (13.5 cm x 28.5 cm), using a rotary cutter and mat and quilter's square to make quick work of the trimming process. Once cut, take a few minutes to decide the layout of your pieces. To make a small throw that measures 33 in x 40 in (82.5 cm x 100 cm), organize the pieces into three rows of eight panels each.

ASSEMBLY

Once you have decided on the perfect layout for your blocks, begin stitching the first row together one-by-one along the 11-in (28.5-cm) edge. To obtain a smoother effect, abut the panels rather than overlapping seams and use a wide zigzag stitch to topstitch them together without excess bulk.

Repeat the process for the second and third rows, then stitch the three rows together in sequence. Take your time and be careful not to stretch your fabrics—gently and evenly feed pieces into your sewing machine without pushing or pulling against the momentum of the feed dogs.

Lightly iron the throw with a gentle steam to relax the panels. Using the drinking glass, place the curve on each corner of the throw and make a tracing. Trim away corners and apply bias tape to finish the edge. (See Baby Burp Cloth, page 28, for more advice on how to apply double fold bias tape.)

MATERIALS

Felted wool in a variety of colors and patterns

5 yds (5 m) double fold bias tape

Thread to match felted wool

EQUIPMENT

Rotary cutter and mat

Quilter's square

Medium-weight to heavyweight ballpoint sewing machine needle

Drinking glass

HELPFUL HINT

To make your own felted wool, wash old 100 percent wool sweaters on the hot water cycle, and tumble dry on high heat. Throw not big enough? Just add rows of blocks to enlarge the size, but remember you will need additional bias tape to edge it.

matchbook sewing kit

This charming kit is easily made up from supplies you have laying around the house. It is perfectly suited for travel, keeping at the office, or gifting. Miles cuter than those ugly throw-away kits from the hotel, this little gem just might make you feel better the next time you lose a button or encounter some other unexpected wardrobe malfunction.

PREPARATION

With pencil, ruler and craft scissors, mark out and cut a piece of heavyweight cardstock measuring 2 in x 3 in (5 cm x 7.5 cm). With a small hole punch, pre-punch a hole on the short side of the card near the edge at the center. Using an awl, make smaller holes in the lower half of the cardstock for the snaps. Gently wrap the sewing threads around the cardstock in between the punched and pierced holes, taking care to keep the card flat and tucking in the thread ends as you go to keep things tidy. Open snaps and attach to card through pre-pierced holes. Stitch spare button to card.

Next, mark out and trim felt to size. Use pinking shears for a pretty, decorative edge. Press matchbook folds into felt. With longest edges oriented top and bottom, measure and fold right side at ⅝ in (1.75 cm). Press with steam using an iron on medium-high heat. Measure and make a second fold 3 in (7.5 cm) from the left side. This edge should fit snuggly under your first fold like a matchbook.

Transfer the embroidery pattern onto the outer side of the 3-in (7.5-cm) section. It can be difficult to transfer images onto felt so you could touch up your design with the disappearing ink marker before you begin embroidering. With embroidery needle and threads, stitch your design into place along the transferred template.

ASSEMBLY

Stitch small closure button into place. It should be centered near the edge of the front cover so that the smaller fold overlaps it. With flap folded over, mark placement of button and snip a buttonhole just smaller than your button into the felt, using very sharp embroidery scissors to give a clean, even opening. Button into place to check fit.

Open cover and insert contents: Align card at left, pinning it into place through the pre-punched hole at the top of the card with a needle. Insert additional straight pins and safety pins into the felt at right. Now you're ready to sew on the go.

MATERIALS

Heavyweight cardstock

Sewing thread in several different shades

Small button to match felt for closure

Sew-in snaps

Wool felt 2¼ in x 6¾ in (6.25 cm x 17.5 cm)

Spare shirt button

Embroidery threads for embellishment

Sewing needle

Straight pins

Safety pins

EQUIPMENT

Pencil

Ruler

Craft scissors

Hole punch

Awl

Pinking shears

Iron and board

Transfer paper and tracing wheel or disappearing ink marker

Embroidery needle for embellishment

Embroidery scissors

HELPFUL HINT

Never embroidered before? Check out the overview in the Hand Stitching and Embroidery section on page 114.

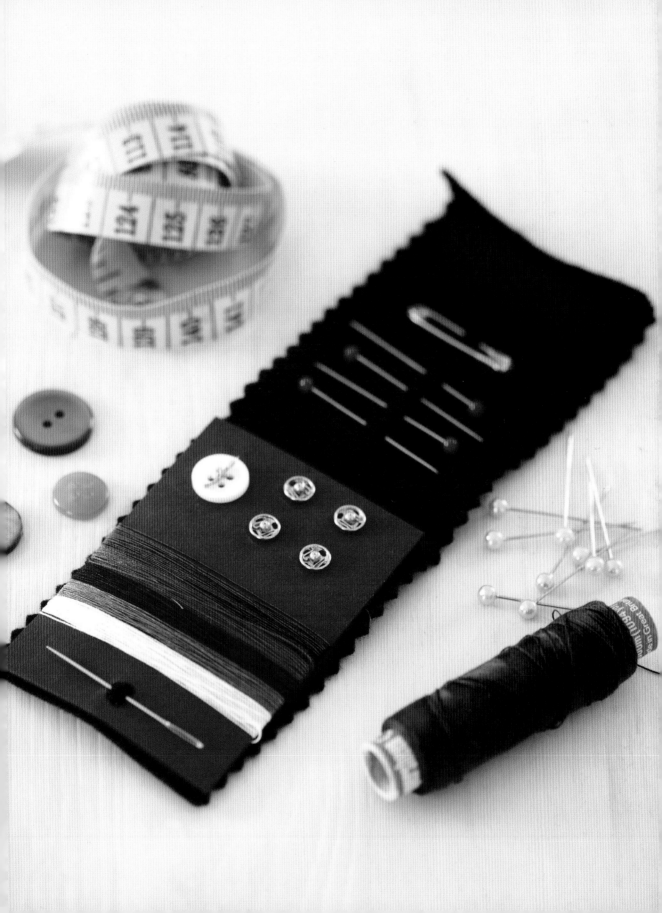

curtains

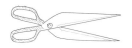

Curtains can change the mood of an entire room with minimum effort. Hanging styles and choices in fabric will help you to create a wide range of looks to suit any taste using this simple pattern. With even the most basic sewing skills, you can create phenomenal designs for the home, so be brave and get ready to update.

MATERIALS

Fabric: A wide variety of fabrics are suitable for curtains—see Preparation for advice on estimating yardage requirements

Thread to match fabric

EQUIPMENT

Yardstick or measuring tape

Tailor's chalk

Fabric scissors

PREPARATION

You will need to do a little bit of measuring and math for this project but once you start to understand the basics of estimation, you will begin to feel more confident in your abilities to take on other sewing challenges.

Take a few measurements to determine the height and width of your window. Your personal preferences should be considered when doing this. How high will your rods hang? Are they mounted inside the casings or above? What is your preferred curtain length? To the sill? To the floor? How full should your curtains be?

First, measure your drop—this is the measurement from the top of your rod to where you would like the panel to end, for example, top of the sill, just below the sill at the edge of the lower casing, to the floor, or "pooling" on the floor. Add 10 in (25 cm) to this measurement—5 in (12.5 cm) for a standard rod pocket and 5 in (12.5 cm) for hemming. You should always double-check that your hardware will accommodate this formula. When measuring brackets, be sure to take the thickness of the rod into account and add a bit of ease so that the pocket will slip easily along the bracketing.

Next, consider the curtain fullness that you would like. For best results, the general rule of thumb for estimating fullness is 1½–2 times the inside width of your windows. Measure the inner width across the casings at both top and bottom as sometimes there are discrepancies, especially with older construction.

My bracket was already mounted to the casing so I opted to leave it in place. The drop from the top of my standard bracket to the top of the sill was 26 in (65 cm) and the inside width of my window was 30 in (75 cm). Because the window was small in size, I opted for less gathering and fullness. Since my window only measured 30-in (75-cm) wide, I selected a fabric with a width of 45 in (110 cm) and opted to split the width length-wise to make two panels from one width. This allowed me to make two 36-in x 22½-in (100-cm x 57-cm) panels from just 1 yd (1 m).

ASSEMBLY

Along either of the longer sides of your fabric lengths, fold edge over by ½ in (1.25 cm) two times. Pin to secure and topstitch along edge. Fold top edge (short side) over by 2½ in (6.25 cm) two times. Pin folded edge

HELPFUL HINT

Before starting, you will need to make a few decisions about the look you are after. This is a very personal choice so consider as many aspects as you can think of that will affect the outcome. How much light do you like? How high are your ceilings? Is your style formal or casual?

and stitch along the edge of the first fold. Do not stitch side openings closed as this is your rod pocket for hanging. Replicate this fold over and stitching at the bottom of the curtain panel for hem and press seams. Repeat process for the second panel and hang.

baby burp cloth

This quick and easy project makes a perfect last-minute baby shower gift. Over the years I've learned that new parents can never have too many burp cloths, so whip up a stack, tie it up in a pretty bow, and prepare to be praised for your handmade prowess.

PREPARATION

Fold fabric in half with wrong sides facing. If fabric width is greater than 44 in (110 cm), trim to size. Trim corners to create a curved edge. An easy trick is to place a drinking glass so that it aligns with either edge at the corner, trace it with tailor's chalk and cut along the traced line.

ASSEMBLY

With cut edges together, pin the wider edge of bias tape into place along the outer edge of the fabric leaving a few inches of bias at the start/finish point. Mark where ends meet and remove pins a few inches back from the start/finish point on either side. Bias tape should be stitched together on an angle for best results so take a little extra time to do this correctly

(see page 108). Overlap bias tape to align your marked end points. Fold and crease under the top tape at a 45-degree angle and mark the bias tape below it along that fold using a disappearing ink marker. Now fold your bias tape out and situate the ends with right sides facing at a 90-degree angle (they should be crossing one another like an "X"). Pin and stitch together so that the 45-degree line that you drew aligns with the crease you made.

Trim excess tape and press seam out. Now re-pin the bias tape back into place along the edge of the fabric and stitch. Fold bias over fabric edge and topstitch tape into position.

(see page 108).

MATERIALS

½ yd (½ m) flannel or other soft fabric

2¼ yds (2¼ m) double fold bias tape

Thread to match fabric

EQUIPMENT

Fabric scissors

Drinking glass

Tailor's chalk or disappearing ink marker

HELPFUL HINT

If you find yourself short on bias tape, you can omit it and simply fold fabric so that right sides are facing. Trim curved edges as described and stitch along outer edge leaving a 2-in (5-cm) opening. Turn work right side out and topstitch. If you have a little more time, consider adding a personal touch and embroider the birth date, name or initials of the new baby.

ribbon wristlet

Worn around the wrist, this beautiful silk bracelet will dress up any outfit with simple elegance. Adapt for a pretty necklace, or to tame tiny tresses, or to wrap a gift in luxury and style—you'll be amazed at how versatile this little accessory is.

MATERIALS

6 yds (6 m) silk ribbon

Thread to match ribbon

2 x small buttons

EQUIPMENT

Hand-sewing needle

PREPARATION

Take time selecting your ribbon. You may want to play with a few samples to determine your preferences with regard to color, width, and drape. These can have a dramatic effect on the final outcome. There is no right or wrong, just preference and taste.

ASSEMBLY

With needle and a length of thread, stitch the first button into place 12–15 in (30–37.5 cm) from one end. With a running stitch, begin working across the length of ribbon in long, even stitches. Gather and compress ribbon together as you go, leaving 12–15 in (30–37.5 cm) at the end of the piece. Compress gathers firmly by pushing toward the first button and knot the thread end to hold gathers in place. Attach second button and trim ribbon ends as required.

HELPFUL HINT

The length and evenness of your stitches determines the bulk and texture of your cuff. Leave ribbon ends a bit longer for a pretty ornamental bow. Wear alone or stacked for more visual impact.

shrug

Softly slipped over your shoulders, this whisper-light shrug will chase the chill of an evening out. Delicate fabric and an open sleeve construction create a feminine drape that feels weightless. Ideal for a romantic fireside evening, or wear casually layered over jeans and a T-shirt to indulge your elegant side.

PREPARATION

Take a modified bust measurement using a measuring tape: Hold one end of the tape in front, wrapping tape under your arms, across your back, and over your chest just above the bust. Make a note of this measurement then subtract 2 in (5 cm). This calculated measurement is the size of your front opening.

Hem the 60-in (150-cm) sides of your fabric with a ¼-in (6-mm) double fold hem (see page 111). With right sides facing, fold panel in half so hemmed edges meet on one side.

Next, center your calculated measurement along the seam opposite the fold and mark the position of your front opening with two pins. Pin the edges together on either side of the center opening to the outer cuffs.

ASSEMBLY

Stitch the two pinned sections together along the previous line of stitches so that the hemmed section is just inside of the seam allowance. Do not stitch the center section closed.

FINISHING

Try your shrug on by slipping your arms through the front opening and into the "sleeves" on either side, gently pulling it into position over your shoulders. Once your shrug is in place, stand with your arms at your sides. Mark your desired sleeve length with a pin just below each wrist and remove garment.

On a flat surface, lay out your shrug so that the stitched seam is to one side. Use your quilter's square and tailor's chalk to mark a line ½ in (1.25 cm) out from the point marked by the pin. With fabric scissors or rotary cutter and quilter's square, trim along marked line and remove excess fabric. Hem the sleeves with a ¼-in (6-mm) double fold hem, similar to that of the neckline.

MATERIALS

1 yd (1 m) 60-in (150-cm) wide lightweight fabric such as silk, voile or velvet

Thread to match fabric

EQUIPMENT

Measuring tape

Quilter's square

Tailor's chalk

Fabric scissors or rotary cutter and mat

HELPFUL HINT

To forego hemming altogether and enjoy this versatile cover up that much quicker, use a large silk scarf (or two of the same size stitched together at center) to make your shrug.

apron

What to do with an old button-down shirt that's worn its way from office to rag pile? This quick and clever restyle will have it back to work as an everyday apron with every bit of boyish charm.

PREPARATION

Using a ruler and disappearing ink marker or tailor's chalk, draw a line on the front of the shirt beginning at the neck where it meets the right shoulder seam to the right underarm of the shirt. Repeat for the left side of the shirt (fig. 1). Turn shirt to backside and draw another line across from underarm to underarm. Next, draw another perpendicular line from the back center point to the underarm line (fig. 2).

Cut away sleeves following the lines you have drawn. Starting at the right underarm seam, trim up the right side to just below the neck seam, then follow this seam around the back to the left side of the garment. Now trim along your markings to the left underarm. Turn work and continue to cut along the underarm line across

the back of the shirt. Take care to trim through the back layer only. If you have done your trimming correctly the sleeves and upper portion will come away leaving the collar attached. Lastly, cut along the center line at the back of the shirt.

ASSEMBLY

Hem the edges on either side of the vertical cut that you made up the back of the shirt and press seams to finish. All other trimmed edges will be finished using your bias tape.

Fold bias tape in half to find center point. Match this point to the center back of the collar and pin into place along either side of the collar, down the front of the shirt and around to the hemmed seams at the back. Topstitch your bias tape into place and finish by pressing seams.

HELPFUL HINT

Check out the Techniques and Skill Builders section on page 108 for tips on applying bias tape and how to make your own in a hurry.

fig. 1   fig. 2

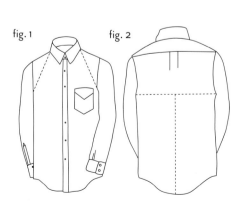

hair accessories

Add a bit of sunshine to an otherwise dreary day with these adorable ornamental bobby pins. Add them to hair elastics for a cute pony tail, or arrange them in multiples on a thin headband or length of ribbon for an inspired way to tame flyaway hair.

PREPARATION

Trace the shape of your button onto felt using a disappearing ink marker. Use pinking shears to cut out about ¼ in (6 mm) outside of the marked line so that the felt peeks out when the button is stitched into place.

ASSEMBLY

Stitch button onto felt shape with embroidery thread. With last few stitches, attach felt piece to the bobby pin near the fold. Knot your thread at the back of the work before trimming.

MATERIALS

An assortment of buttons

Small pieces of wool felt in assorted colors

Embroidery thread

Bobby pins

EQUIPMENT

Disappearing ink marker

Pinking shears

Hand-sewing needle

HELPFUL HINT

This makes a great first time sewing project for kids.

hair band

Hair trends come and go but a pretty headband is always in style. Whip up a few in no time flat and transform frizzy flyaway hair into posh locks with this fashion classic.

PREPARATION

A headband should always stretch to fit so you will want to make it just a bit smaller than your actual head measurements. To get the best fit, measure the circumference of your head. Since the edges of this pattern fold over 1 in (2.5 cm) on either end, you will lose about 2 in (5 cm) overall, which is perfect for final sizing. If you are using a ribbon, you will only need to trim length to size. If you are using fabric, you will also need to decide on your desired width, adding ½ in (1.25 cm) to it for seam allowance.

Here is an example of the formula you will use to cut your fabric to size. The circumference of my head measures 22 in (55 cm) and I want a 3-in (7.5-cm) width for my headband, so I cut my fabric pieces 22 in x 3½ in (55 cm x 8.75 cm), which allows for a seam allowance of ¼ in (6 mm).

Now using your own calculations, mark out and cut two pieces of fabric. For variety, I used complementary fabrics on either side to achieve two looks with one headband.

ASSEMBLY

To make a ribbon headband, fold ribbon over the elastic then tuck unfinished ends back into the fold and topstitch into place. Repeat at other end.

To make a fabric headband, stitch fabrics together with right sides facing, leaving a 2-in (5-cm) opening along one edge for turning work right side out. Turn work and press panel along seams. Stitch opening shut. Next fold panel 1 in (2.5 cm) from the end, insert elastic under flap and topstitch down. Repeat at other end so that both ends are attached to the elastic in a loop.

MATERIALS

¼ yd (¼ m) medium-weight fabric or ¾ yd (¾ m) ribbon

Large 2-in (5-cm) diameter hair elastic

Thread to match fabric or ribbon

EQUIPMENT

Measuring tape

Tailor's chalk or disappearing ink marker

Fabric scissors

HELPFUL HINT

To make the luxury spa variation on the left, substitute terry cloth for one of your fabrics and add 4 in (10 cm) to the length. Trim rounded edges at either end of wrap and stitch panels together with right sides facing. Omit the hair elastic and install 2 in (5 cm) of Velcro on either side of overlapping edges. This version is perfect for washing rituals and at-home facials.

obi belt

Universally flattering, this waist-defining, wide-sash belt can add structure to a longer silhouette, and it provides a pop of color or a dramatic flourish to any outfit. This multi-faceted accessory will wrap, twist or cinch your wardrobe from totally drab into utterly fab.

PREPARATION

First, use a measuring tape to take your waist measurement (see Taking Measurements, page 105). Cut two panels, one from each of the coordinating fabrics, measuring 6 in (15 cm) x your waist measurement.

With right sides facing, fold each piece of fabric in half so shorter edges meet. Use a drinking glass and tailor's chalk or disappearing ink marker to mark rounded edges at each corner. Trim corners along marked lines cutting through both layers. Unfold the fabric pieces to reveal newly rounded edges. Align panels with right sides facing and check that your curves match at each corner. Cut ribbon in half to give you two 1-yd (1-m) lengths.

ASSEMBLY

Sandwich ribbons between fabrics at the center of either end of the sash and pin in place. To ensure that you do not catch ties in seams as you stitch your main panels together, you may want to secure the loose ends of the ribbons at this point by folding them into the center of the work and pinning. Pin edges of the fabric panel together and stitch around outer edge leaving a 2–3-in (5–7.5-cm) opening on one side to turn work right side out. Remove pins and turn work by pulling ribbons from the inside out.

Press seams flat and use blind stitch to sew opening closed. Time to try it on—holding sash against the front of your waist, cross ribbons around the back, and tie in a bow at the front.

MATERIALS

¼ yd (¼ m) each of two coordinating fabrics

2 yds (2 m) ½-in (1.25-cm) wide ribbon

Thread to match fabrics

EQUIPMENT

Measuring tape

Fabric scissors

Drinking glass

Tailor's chalk or disappearing ink marker

Straight pins

Hand-sewing needles

stuffed owls

Hoot. Hoot. Otto loves his tree house home in the woods and wants to remind you to be kind to the earth by recycling and reusing everyday items. Get creative and do your part by repurposing those old, felted sweaters into something special. Stuff him with wool batting to create a snuggly, earth-friendly toy for your favorite little one.

INTERMEDIATE

SEE TEMPLATES ON PAGE 116

MATERIALS

Felted sweater scraps

1–2 oz (30–60 g) wool batting

Several yards (meters) of yarn

EQUIPMENT

Craft and fabric scissors

Straight pins

Hand-sewing needle with large eye

HELPFUL HINT

If you plan to use your owl as a pincushion, weight it with craft beads in addition to stuffing with wool batting.

PREPARATION

Photocopy or transfer the templates on page 116 to pattern paper. Lay out and cut pattern pieces from felted sweaters as marked on the pattern paper.

ASSEMBLY

Fold bottom corners of the ear pieces to the center and pin between body panels aligning center point to marks on either side. Beginning at lower right-hand edge and working around to the lower left, whip stitch panels together using yarn. Take special care to take needle through all three layers at ear panels, and be sure to leave bottom section open for insert panel.

Next, fold the eye panel in half so that it bisects the beak, and whip stitch the beak edges together. Press beak up into a three-dimensional shape with your fingers. Attach the eye panel to the main body panel: Working clockwise from upper center point of the panel, attach eyes through front body panel only with large, evenly-spaced stitches that stretch from the outer edge to a single convergence point at the center of each eye.

Stuff owl firmly with wool batting. Place insert panel into the opening at the bottom of the owl body and whip stitch body cavity closed. Arrange the wing overlays on top of the wing panels and stitch the layered pieces to the front of the body as one.

◄ projects

cat tent

Pitch perfect fun for furry friends—this little lean-to makes for loads of environmental enrichment at home as cats love to explore, and its collapsible design makes it easy to take the show on the road.

PREPARATION

Cut four pieces 45 in x 18 in (112.5 cm x 45 cm), two of main color (MC) fabric, one of contrasting color (CC) fabric, and one of batting. Cut five ribbon ties 4 in (10 cm) each.

ASSEMBLY

Begin by sandwiching batting panel between CC panel and one of the MC panels, so that the right sides of fabric panels are facing out from the batting at center. Using your sewing machine's walking foot, quilt the three layers together. Next, mark a line 15 in (37.5 cm) from end of the second MC fabric panel and cut the panel in two (one panel will measure 18 in x 15 in/45 cm x 37.5 cm, the other 18 in x 30 in/45 cm x 75 cm).

Apply bias tape to each of the panels along the edge of the cut you just made. Abut panels so that bias tape is aligned and stay stitch across bias on either end to reconnect panels leaving the bias edge open.

Place the bisected MC panel over matching side of quilted panel and pin layers together. Stitch layers together with a single line 15 in (37.5 cm) in from end *and* 15 in (37.5 cm) from opening. Next, apply bias tape around outer edge of entire panel, inserting ribbon ties as you go. Attach two of the precut ribbons evenly spaced at 6 in (15 cm) and 12 in (30 cm) along one side of bias tape opening, and add buttons to align on the other side of the opening. Attach remaining ribbons at 3 in (7.5 cm), 9 in (22.5 cm), and 18 in (45 cm) along the outer edge of the panel, parallel to opening. Sew three buttons into place at the opposite end of the panel to align with these ties.

Insert the two pieces of cardboard into the bias opening and tie ribbon to close. Fold cardboard walls into peak, then slip quilted panel underneath. Secure quilted panel base in place by wrapping ribbons around corresponding buttons.

HELPFUL HINT

When traveling, bring your tent along and set it up in a quiet corner when you arrive. It provides the soothing scent of home and offers a place for your pet to camp out and acclimate to a new place.

juggling balls

Acrobats, clowns, and monkeys too! Bring home the Big Top with this set of colorful jugglers. With a little bit of concentration, considerable silliness, and a whole lot of practice, you'll be ready for the spotlight.

PREPARATION

Transfer the juggling ball template on page 117 to plain paper and cut out. Lay out and cut three fabric panels for each ball (panels 1, 2, and 3)—to make a juggling set (minimum three balls), cut out at least nine panels.

ASSEMBLY

With right sides facing, stitch panels 1 and 2 together along one seam. Next align panel 3 with panel 2 and stitch together along common seam. Align remaining unstitched edges of panels 1 and 3, and stitch together with right sides facing leaving a 1-in (2.5-cm) opening. Turn work right side out. Fill with flax seed and stitch opening closed along seam.

SEE TEMPLATE ON PAGE 117

HELPFUL HINT

Tiny hands? The template for this pattern can easily be sized up or down using a photocopier or scanner. Create juggling sets in a variety of dimensions or make a small single ball for a rousing game of hacky sack.

MATERIALS

¼ yd (¼ m) each of three medium-weight to heavyweight cotton fabrics.

Thread to match fabrics

Flax seed

EQUIPMENT

Transfer paper and tracing wheel

Plain paper

Craft and fabric scissors

INTERMEDIATE

tic-tac-toe

Everybody loves a game of tic-tac-toe—perfect for camping, long road trips, or a rainy afternoon. When they're done, collect and keep game pieces tidy and organized inside the drawstring game-board bag.

PREPARATION

Measure and cut two panels of game-board bag fabric to 11½ in x 14 in (28.75 cm x 35 cm). Measure and cut 10 squares from each of the contrasting game-piece fabrics to 3 in x 3 in (7.5 cm x 7.5 cm), to give you a total of 20 fabric pieces. Cut the game-board ribbon to two lengths of 14 in (35 cm) each and two lengths of 11½ in (28.75 cm).

ASSEMBLY

game pieces

Using matching fabrics, position two pieces with right sides facing and seam together leaving a 1½ in (3.75 cm) opening to turn work. Clip corners, turn panels right side out, and press seams. Fill game piece with flax seed and stitch closed. Repeat to make 10 playing pieces (five per team).

game-board bag

Place the game-board panels on a flat surface, right side up with short side at top. Using tailor's chalk and a ruler, measure and mark a line 2½ in (6.25 cm) from the top edge on each piece.

Set aside one panel and continue board layout on the other panel as follows: Measure and mark a second line 3¾ in (9.5 cm) below the first line, and a third line 3¾ in (9.5 cm) below the second. Rotate fabric 90

degrees (the longer side is now at the top). Measure and mark a line 3¾ in (9.5 cm) below the top edge, then mark a second line 3¾ in (9.5 cm) below the first line.

With right side facing, center and pin corresponding ribbon lengths along all but the first line marked out, so that the ribbons stretch the full length of the panel. Topstitch along both edges of each ribbon to secure.

With wrong sides facing, align the game-board panels with the remaining 2½ in (6.25 cm) marking at the top. Leaving this end open, stitch panels together along the other three sides with a ¼-in (6-mm) seam allowance. Clip stitched corners, turn work inside out, and press seams. Stitch along seam again using a ½-in (1.25 cm) seam allowance to enclose cut edges in a French seam. Turn work right side out.

Measure in 1 in (2.5 cm) from the left seam and mark out a 1-in (2.5-cm) buttonhole in the 2½-in (6.25-cm) area you marked out earlier. Stitch buttonhole into place and cut away fabric at the center to open hole.

To create a drawstring casing, fold unfinished edge to wrong side to first marked line and press. Fold fabric over again, press seam, and edge-stitch to complete.

Attach safety pin to one end of remaining length of ribbon. Insert safety pin into the drawstring casing

HELPFUL HINT

When little ones outgrow the traditional version of this game, keep things interesting with tic-tac-toss, where teams take turns tossing their pieces into place.

through the buttonhole, and pull ribbon through opening and back out the buttonhole. Trim and tie ribbon ends together to secure.

crayon caddy

Scribble, doodle, count, and draw. Keep crayons neatly organized and ready for on-the-go fun anytime. This pocket-sized wonder will challenge and engage wee ones with the endless possibilities of imaginative play.

PREPARATION

Cut two pieces of fabric 11 in x 15 in (27.5 cm x 37.5 cm) to match batting.

ASSEMBLY

Position the fabric panels with right sides facing so that edges align, then place batting on top. Pin layers together. Measure and mark fabric 5 in (12.5 cm) from corner along the shorter side. With a ½-in (1.25-cm) seam allowance, stitch from marked point along the outer edge of the layered panel leaving a 2-in (5-cm) opening at the end of your seam to turn work. Clip the corners. Reach between the two fabric panels to pull the corners through the opening so right side of work is facing out. Press along seams.

Cut elastic to length—it should be just long enough to stretch over the button when folded and stitched into the seam. Fold elastic in half and position cut ends into the opening so that they line up with the unfinished edge inside. Pin in place.

Position your work so that the elastic tab is on the upper right-hand side. Now measure 2½ in (6.25 cm) from bottom edge and fold up. Pin in place and press fold. Topstitch around outer edge and backstitch over the elastic to be sure it is firmly attached.

To make the crayon pockets, measure and mark out 1-in (2.5-cm) sections along the long edges of the fabric panel, working in from each side and leaving a larger pocket at the center. I made five sections on either side leaving space for a 4-in x 6-in (10-cm x 15-cm) doodle pad. Topstitch along marked lines using backstitch or lock stitch at the top of the pocket for added stitch strength.

Fold the caddy in thirds and attach the button so that it aligns with the elastic loop.

MATERIALS

⅓ yd (⅓ m) medium-weight fabric

Batting 11 in x 15 in (27.5 cm x 37.5 cm)

⅛ yd (⅛ m) ¼-in (6-mm) wide elastic

Thread to match fabric

Button

EQUIPMENT

Fabric scissors

Measuring tape, yardstick or quilter's square

Straight pins

Tailor's chalk or disappearing ink marker

HELPFUL HINT

If corners still seem bulky after clipping, trim away a little bit more just along the sides. Be careful not to trim too closely though, and be gentle turning corners so you don't tear out seams.

door sign

Express yourself with this versatile message board. Use it to label and organize, offer reminders to wash hands, request privacy for study, or quietly profess words of love. Follow this recipe to make adorable adaptations for any room.

PREPARATION

Disassemble embroidery hoop into two pieces. Place your fabric and Chalkcloth face down on a flat surface, and trace around the inner (smaller) hoop of the embroidery frame. Cut out with a ½-in (1.25-cm) seam allowance around marked lines.

ASSEMBLY

With right sides facing, stitch fabrics together along marked line around half the circumference, leaving enough space to insert the inner (smaller) hoop between the fabric and Chalkcloth. Turn work right side out and insert inner hoop, then close opening with blind stitch. Take your time and be sure to stitch the piece together with enough pressure to maintain a taut, drum-like stretch to fabrics for best results. Place the larger outer hoop over the smaller hoop—now enclosed in fabric—unscrewing nut at top as needed to accommodate the added bulk of the fabric panels. Attach ribbon through screw mechanism at top and hang.

MATERIALS

½ yd (½ m) Chalkcloth

½ yd (½ m) lightweight contrasting fabric

2 yds (2 m) 1-in (2.5-cm) wide ribbon

Heavy-duty thread to match fabric

Embroidery hoop in size of your choosing

EQUIPMENT

Fabric scissors

Disappearing ink marker or tailor's chalk

HELPFUL HINT

Embroidery hoops come in a variety of sizes and are inexpensive, so consider using a few for a decorative touch with minimal effort. Precut fabrics, then add family and friends for a wonderful activity or party favor.

growth chart

Childhood passes in the blink of an eye, so take the time to chart the special moments in development along the way. This darling project introduces the basics of quilting and makes a lovely gift for a baby shower or for a newborn baby.

PREPARATION

Measure and cut front panels to size as follows: Cut one piece of striped fabric 5 in x 1⅔ yds (12.5 cm x 1⅔ m) and one piece of coordinating fabric 12 in x 1⅔ yds (30 cm x 1⅔ m). Cut one backing panel 16 in x 1⅔ yds (40 cm x 1⅔ m) from coordinating fabric. Cut grosgrain ribbon in half to make two 18 in (50 cm) pieces.

ASSEMBLY

With right sides facing, align the two front panels so that they are matched to one side and pin in place. Stitch panels together along the longest edge and press seam out.

Next, sandwich batting between the assembled front panel and backing piece so that right sides are facing out. Pin or baste these three layers together. Attach walking foot and quilt layers together—be sure to stitch lines in sequence across the panel, beginning at the same edge with each pass for best results.

Measure and mark the top edge of your quilted panel 1½ in (3.75 cm) from each corner to mark ribbon positions. Use a drinking glass to mark out a curved edge at each corner (top and bottom) and trim. Fold cut ribbons in half. Position

ribbons on the back side of your panel at marked positions so the folds are aligned to the edge. Baste ribbons in place.

Apply bias tape over the outer edge. Your bias tape should only overlap the fold of the ribbons; you may want to pin ribbon to the back of your panel to ensure the cut ends are not accidentally sewn into the biased edge.

If you have never applied bias tape before, see Techniques and Skill Builders, page 108.

Tie each ribbon into a bow and hang.

MATERIALS

1⅔ yds (1⅔ m) horizontal striped fabric

1⅔ yds (1⅔ m) coordinating fabric

1 yd (1 m) ½-in (1.25-cm) wide grosgrain ribbon for hanging

1⅔ yds (1⅔ m) cotton batting

Thread to match fabrics

5¾ yds (5¾ m) ½-in (1.25-cm) bias tape

EQUIPMENT

Quilter's square

Tailor's chalk

Fabric scissors

Walking foot

Drinking glass

HELPFUL HINT

This chart can be marked with a permanent fabric pen or information can be stitched onto the panel with embroidery thread. Include a fine fabric marker or a small sewing kit when gifting this heirloom.

bleacher seat

Whether you're in the stands cheering for the home team, fireside at the campsite, or resting along the trail, this little fold-up is a friend indeed. Just a bit of padded protection from the elements, it will keep your seat comfy and dry.

PREPARATION

Cut four panels from your fabric, each 13 in x 17 in (32.5 cm x 42.5 cm), and round corners if desired. Cut two pieces of foam to match fabric size. Fold ribbon in half and cut (measures 27 in/67.5 cm).

ASSEMBLY

Baste bias tape into place along the edge on the right side of the first panel, stitching ends of bias together at a 45-degree angle (see page 108). With wrong sides facing, align the second panel to the first and stitch together along the bias basting line, leaving a 6-in (15-cm) opening. Insert foam through this opening, smooth into place, and seam opening shut.

Fold one of the precut ribbons in half. Place fold at center point along edge of one of the shorter sides of the panel and pin in place so that bias tape folds over the ribbon at the fold. Topstitch bias tape into place.

On the long sides of the cushion, measure and mark three lines that bisect it in equal sections. Topstitch through all three layers along marked lines to create defined folding points in the seat. Fold seat accordion style, and wrap with ribbon ties to secure.

Repeat process to make a second seat.

HELPFUL HINT

Once your foam is installed, you will want to switch to a heavy-duty needle and walking foot to help feed bulky materials through your machine smoothly. Always let the machine do the work. Never push, pull, or force materials through as it could cause needle breakage or damage to your machine.

MATERIALS

To make two fold-up seats:

¾ yd (¾ m) medium-weight to heavyweight fabric

¾ yd (¾ m) foam or padding ½-in (1.25-cm) thick

1½ yds (1½ m) grosgrain ribbon

4 yds (4 m) double fold bias tape

Heavy-duty thread to match fabric

EQUIPMENT

Fabric scissors

Measuring tape, yardstick or quilter's square

Straight pins

Walking foot

Heavy-duty or denim machine-sewing needle

INTERMEDIATE

picnic blanket

Picnics in the park, concerts on the lawn, or a day at the beach. Whatever your pleasure, this bring-along blanket is always the best seat in the house. A Chalkcloth backing provides an additional barrier against ground moisture and keeps the kids entertained to boot.

PREPARATION

Cut cotton fabric, batting and Chalkcloth to size, each measuring 45 in x 60 in (112.5 cm x 150 cm). Mark webbing 18 in (45 cm) from end and cut.

ASSEMBLY

Place batting between fabric and Chalkcloth so right sides are facing out and edges are aligned. Baste panels together around outer edge.

Measure 18 in (45 cm) in from the corner along one of the 60-in (150-cm) sides of the blanket, and pin one end of the shorter length of strapping into place, so that the cut edge aligns with the edge of the panel. Position the other end of the strapping 6 in (15 cm) from the first and pin in place. Attach the remaining strap to the edge so that it abuts the outside edges of the first strap attached. Baste straps along your previous stitch line. Pin and stitch bias tape into place over the edge of the blanket to finish.

Fold blanket in half and roll as you would a sleeping bag, so that the straps end up on the outside. Wrap the longer strap around the outside of the blanket and pass it through the smaller loop to secure the bundle.

MATERIALS

1⅔ yd (1⅔ m) Chalkcloth, oilcloth or vinyl

1⅔ yd (1⅔ m) medium-weight to heavyweight cotton fabric

1⅔ yd (1⅔ m) cotton batting

2 yds (2 m) 1-in (2.5-cm) wide cotton webbing

6½ yds (6½ m) double fold bias tape

Heavy-duty thread to match fabric

EQUIPMENT

Fabric scissors

Measuring tape, yardstick or quilter's square

Disappearing ink marker or tailor's chalk

Straight pins

Walking foot

Leather sewing machine needle

HELPFUL HINT

To speed things along and avoid wrestling with bulky seams, use a walking foot and leather needle for this project.

throw pillows

Formal meets fun in this cheeky nod to a tuxedo that's anything but stuffy. Sophisticated soiree or casual cocktail party, this mix-and-match pillow pair will have you red-carpet ready before the paparazzi arrive.

ruffled pillow

PREPARATION

From main fabric cut one front panel 18 in x 18 in (45 cm x 45 cm), two backing panels 13 in x 18 in (32.5 cm x 45 cm), and one ruffle panel 6 in x 44 in (15 cm x 110 cm). From coordinating fabric cut one ruffle panel 6 in x 44 in (15 cm x 110 cm).

ASSEMBLY

With right sides facing, stitch the two ruffle panels together leaving a 2-in (5-cm) opening. Turn work right side out through opening, press seams, and stitch opening closed. Stitch two parallel basting lines at center along the length of ruffle panel and gather fabric to 18 in (45 cm). Position ruffle left of center on the right side of the front panel and stitch into place. Use a seam ripper to gently remove basting stitches. See page 111 for advice on creating ruffles.

Apply bias tape along one 18-in (45-cm) edge of the backing panels. If you do not have bias tape, simply hem the edge by folding over twice and stitching along the folded edge.

With right sides facing, pin backing panels into place on top of the front panel so that finished edges

overlap at center and the ends of the ruffled edge are secured in the outer seam. Stitch all the way around the outside edge. If you have a bit more time, consider finishing inside seams with bias tape.

Turn cover right side out and attach buttons evenly along center of ruffle if desired. Insert pillow form.

color block cushion

PREPARATION

From main fabric, measure and cut two back panels 18 in x 13 in (45 cm x 32.5 cm) and one front panel 12 in x 18 in (30 cm x 45 cm). Cut one front panel 7 in x 18 in (17.5 cm x 45 cm) from your coordinating fabric.

ASSEMBLY

With right sides facing, sandwich grosgrain ribbon between the two front panels. Pin along edge and stitch layers together with ¼-in (6-mm) seam allowance. Hem or finish edges of back panels with bias tape as for ruffled pillow. Position back panels so that they overlap at center and stitch into place around outer edge. Finish inner seams with bias tape if desired. Turn cover right side out and insert pillow form.

MATERIALS

To make one throw pillow:

½ yd (½ m) medium-weight to heavyweight main cotton fabric

¼ yd (¼ m) medium-weight to heavyweight coordinating cotton fabric

6–8 x shirt buttons for ruffled pillow only (optional)

½ yd (½ m) ½-in (1.25-cm) wide grosgrain ribbon for color block cushion only

Double fold bias tape (optional)

Thread to match fabrics

Pillow form 18 in x 18 in (45 cm x 45 cm)

EQUIPMENT

Fabric scissors

Ruler, measuring tape or quilter's square

Seam ripper

Straight pins

eye mask

Restful and uninterrupted sleep is an essential ingredient for health and well-being. Travel, stress, or other unexpected situations can make it difficult to relax and slumber. Perfectly suited to nightly sleeping, cat naps or restful meditation, this mask will block unwanted light and distractions, allowing you to relax and recharge in peace.

PREPARATION

Using the eye mask template on page 117, cut two pieces from fabric and one piece from batting.

ASSEMBLY

If you like a decorative edge, begin by pinning rick rack to the right side of one of the fabric pieces all along the outer edge. Baste into place along the center of the rick rack tape.

Cut elastic to 14 in (36.5 cm). This length fits most, but you can add a bit of length if needed. Remember: The size of the completed mask should be a bit smaller than the recipient's head, so that it will stretch into place properly. Pin elastic into place on the right side of the panel to which you applied the rick rack, taking time to center it on either side. Baste into place along the same stitch line to which you secured the rick rack.

Place the two fabric panels together with right sides facing. Align batting piece on top so shaping matches, then pin layers together. The elastic will be inside the bundle so be careful not to pin (or stitch) it into the seam.

Starting at the top center, stitch all three layers together, leaving a 2-in (5-cm) opening to turn work right side out. I usually follow the basting line to be sure it disappears into the seam, and this also avoids having to remove the basting stitches.

Clip out small triangular sections of the seam allowance in the curved area around the nose (this will allow fabric to stretch and lay flat). Take care not to over-clip or cut through the seam when you do this. Turn work right side out, press, and stitch opening closed.

SEE TEMPLATE ON PAGE 117

MATERIALS
¼ yd (¼ m) medium-weight cotton fabric

¾ yd (¾ m) rick rack (optional)

½ yd (½ m) decorative or fold-over elastic

¼ yd (¼ m) cotton batting

Thread to match fabric

EQUIPMENT
Craft and fabric scissors

Straight pins

HELPFUL HINT
For a cooling spa mask variation, omit the batting and instead lightly fill mask with flax seed. The completed mask can be stored in the freezer in a sealable plastic bag until needed. Apply for 15 minutes to relieve puffy and fatigued eyes.

pincushion

This useful tailor's tool makes a wonderful gift for stitchers. Three variations keep pins sharp and handy whatever your pinning preferences. Make a traditional tabletop version, add an elastic band and wear it around your wrist, or secure it to your sewing machine with a pretty bow.

PREPARATION

Select one of the two sizes and transfer the pattern template to fabric. Cut two panels.

ASSEMBLY

With right side facing, apply bias tape or rick rack along the edge of one of the panel pieces if desired. If you are making the wristlet or sewing machine option, pin a length of elastic or ribbon into place at either side with raw edges together. Next, with right sides facing, align the panel pieces together and stitch into place leaving a 1-in (2.5-cm) opening. Turn work right side out, stuff firmly with wool stuffing or craft beads, and stitch opening closed. If desired embellish with a button at the center.

SEE TEMPLATES ON PAGE 118

MATERIALS

¼ yd (¼ m) medium-weight to heavyweight cotton fabric

½ yd (½ m) bias tape or rick rack (optional)

¾ yd (¾ m) ribbon or ¼ yd (¼ m) elastic

Wool stuffing

Craft beads (optional for weight)

Button (optional)

EQUIPMENT

Tailor's chalk or transfer paper and tracing wheel

Straight pins

HELPFUL HINT

Experiment with this pattern to come up with fun variations, and remember to stuff your pincushion with wool to keep your pins sharp and rust free.

wall pockets

How does your garden grow? This hanging plant pocket is a wonderful solution for urban gardeners short on space. Whether it's herbs in the kitchen or daffodils on the deck, it's time to dig in the dirt and see what takes root.

PREPARATION

Using your quilter's square, lay out oilcloth panels to the following sizes: Three pieces 12 x 7½ in (30 x 18.75 cm) and one 12 x 47 in (30 x 117.5 cm). Cut out using craft scissors. Attach bias tape along one of the long sides of each of the three smaller panels (panels 1, 2, and 3).

ASSEMBLY

Fold the larger oilcloth panel in half with wrong sides facing and find the center point at 23½ in (58.75 cm). Measure and mark a line in the seam allowance on each side of the backing panel 3 in (7.5 cm) from the fold. Unfold the panel and place the biased edge of panel 1 so that it is aligned to the marks. Stitch the panel into place along the three unfinished edges. Next, lay out panels 2 and 3 in sequence so that the biased edge overlaps the bottom edge of the panel before it by 1 in (2.5 cm), stitching each panel into place before placing the next panel over it (see diagram).

Apply bias around outer edge of assembled panel to finish edges. Fold panel in half with wrong sides facing and the shorter edges aligned. Pin layers together through the biased edge and stitch together leaving a ½-in (1.25-cm) opening at the fold to insert the hanging dowel.

MATERIALS
⅓ yd (⅓ m) oilcloth

6 yds (6 m) double fold bias tape

⅜-in (1-cm) dowel diameter cut to 12 in (30 cm)

2 x small eye screws

½ yd (½ m) ribbon

EQUIPMENT
Quilter's square

Craft and fabric scissors

Straight pins

HELPFUL HINT
Be sure to do your pinning for this project in the seam allowance only, to avoid holes in your oilcloth.

Twist an eye screw into place at each end, and slip the dowel into the opening at the top of the work. Tie ribbon through the eye screws on each end of the dowel and hang.

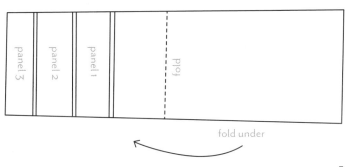

panel 3 · panel 2 · panel 1 · fold

fold under

glasses case

Gloriously geeky or ultra-chic, this soft carrying case will keep sunglasses or spectacles safe from scratches and rough treatment while in transit. Stitch up a few for tons of four-eyed fun...

INTERMEDIATE

PREPARATION

Using the glasses case template on page 118, cut four pieces from fabric and four pieces from cotton batting.

ASSEMBLY

Sandwich two pieces of batting between two pieces of fabric, so that the right sides of the fabric are facing out on either side of the batting and edges are aligned. Baste layers together with contrasting thread. Repeat with the remaining fabric/batting pieces.

Cut a 1½-in (3.75-cm) piece of bias tape and topstitch open edge of bias closed. Fold strip in half so that cut edges meet to form a loop and pin in place at the center top opening along one of the shorter edges of one of the basted panels. The cut edges of the bias tape should be aligned with the cut edge of the fabric panel, so that the raw edges are stitched into the seam allowance when the bias tape is applied.

Apply bias around the outer edge of each of the two basted panels. If you have never worked with bias tape before, review the bias tape tutorial in the Techniques and Skill Builders section on page 108. Pin the two panels together, then topstitch along three sides leaving the top edge (looped side) open.

Stitch button into place across from loop at top of case. The loop should slip over the button with a firm fit.

SEE TEMPLATE ON PAGE 118

MATERIALS

¼ yd (¼ m) medium-weight cotton fabric

¼ yd (¼ m) cotton batting

1 yd (1 m) ¼-in (6-mm) double fold bias tape

½-in (1.25-cm) diameter button to match fabric

Thread to match fabric and contrast color

EQUIPMENT

Craft and fabric scissors

Straight pins

Hand-sewing needle

HELPFUL HINT

Consider substituting a soft microfiber cloth for the inner lining panels for maximum functionality.

tote bag

Transform the most basic of recyclables into something sustainable with this ingenious pattern sourced from a humble brown-paper bag. So pretty and versatile, you're sure to use this clever tote for more than weekly trips to the market.

PREPARATION

With craft scissors, cut paper bag in half along side seam, across the bottom, and up the other side. Next, cut along fold to corner on either side of one of the pieces, and fold out flat. This is your pattern template.

Using your pattern template, cut two pieces from each of the fabrics to give you four panels.

Measure and cut the webbing into two 24-in (60-cm) lengths.

ASSEMBLY

Place one of the panels right side up on a flat surface and fold the bottom left cut out in so edges meet to form a corner. Pin in place and stitch together. Repeat at bottom right. Clip corners and press seams open. Repeat process on remaining panels.

Match like fabric panels. With right sides facing, stitch together along center seam, then press seams open. Repeat. You should now have two unfinished "bags." Turn one bag right side out and insert the other into it (wrong sides facing). Aligning side seams, fold edges in ½ in (1.25 cm), and press fold.

Next, position webbing evenly on one side of the bag and pin ends into

place between layers. You may want to baste strap ends to one side before pinning layers together. Attach second strap and check its position to be sure it mirrors the placement of the first strap before basting. Finally, topstitch around the top edge to finish.

MATERIALS

Brown-paper grocery bag

⅔ yd (⅔ m) each of two coordinating medium-weight to heavyweight cotton fabrics

1⅓ yd (1⅓ m) 2-in (5-cm) wide cotton webbing

Thread to match fabric

EQUIPMENT

Craft and fabric scissors

Disappearing ink marker

Straight pins

reversible clutch

The vintage style of wooden handles is twice as nice with the reversible design of this classic clutch. Make a statement—or two—with this stylish accessory that has just enough space for everyday essentials and plenty of personality to help you stand out in the crowd.

PREPARATION

Position the sheet of paper horizontally on a flat surface. Use a drinking glass to mark out a curved line in each of the bottom corners, and trim paper along marked lines using craft scissors.

With right side facing, fold one of your fabrics in half, and match the bottom edge of your pattern piece to the fabric fold. Trace along the outer edge of your paper template with tailor's chalk. With fabric scissors, cut through both layers of the fabric along the marked line taking extra care to leave the fold intact. Repeat process with contrasting fabric for second panel.

ASSEMBLY

On a flat surface, unfold the fabric panels, placing one over the other with right sides facing, so that the outer edges of each panel are perfectly aligned. Pin edges and stitch fabrics together leaving a 2–3-in (5–7.5-cm) opening at the center of one of the straight edges. Trim fabric in each corner and notch curves, then turn work right side out—use a point protector or knitting needle to gently turn corners if needed. Press seams and stitch opening closed.

Fold straight fabric edges over opening in each handle and pin in place—some gathering should occur. Topstitch fabric around handles.

INTERMEDIATE

MATERIALS

⅓ yd (⅓ m) each of two coordinating medium-weight or heavyweight fabrics

Pair of wooden bag handles 7-in (17.5-cm) wide

Thread to match fabrics

EQUIPMENT

Sheet of plain paper 8½ in x 11 in (21.25 cm x 27.5 cm)

Pencil

Tailor's chalk

Drinking glass

Craft and fabric scissors

Straight pins

HELPFUL HINT

If you have time when attaching the handles, consider applying a line of 3–4 buttonholes along the straight edge and corresponding buttons on either side of the fold over, for a quick change option that is easy to remove for laundering.

halter top

Effortless summer style is a breeze with this delicately draped pattern. Create a stylish beach-to-shopping cover up, a chic and sophisticated shift for your next summer soiree, or shorten things up for a cute blouse.

PREPARATION

You will first need to determine your measurements. If you have never taken measurements before, check out the Taking Measurements tutorial on page 105 for a bit of visual guidance.

Measure yourself at the widest part of your hip and bust. Record your measurements. To determine the length of your garment, stand with good posture in front of a mirror, and hold the measuring tape just above left or right bust at your desired neckline. Allow the tape to drape freely over your bust to the floor. Do not bend or stoop to read the measurement, but instead use your reflection to make a note of your desired length. Record this measurement.

If hip or bust measurement is wider than 42 in (105 cm), be sure to purchase a fabric with a 60-in (150-cm) width. Determine the yardage you will need by adding 4 in (10 cm) to the desired length measurement noted.

ASSEMBLY

Fold your fabric with selvedges together, and cut in half along fold. Square your fabric and trim to size leaving fabric width (44 in/110 cm or 60 in/150 cm) intact. Remember: Your length measurement will be 4 in (10 cm) longer than desired finished length.

Position your fabric panels with wrong sides facing so that selvedge edge is along the right side. Now, measure 10 in (25 cm) down from top right corner along selvedge edge and mark with a pin. Next, measure 6 in (15 cm) from top right corner along the top edge and mark with a pin. Using a ruler and tailor's chalk, connect the marked

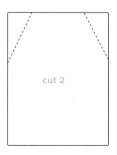

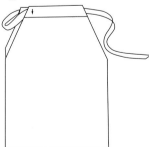

fig. 1

cut 2

fig. 2

points. Repeat at top left corner. Cut through both panels along the marked lines (see fig. 1).

Along each of the diagonal lines just cut, fold the fabric over twice to press a ¼-in (6-mm) hem and topstitch at edge.

With wrong sides facing, stitch panels together with a ¼-in (6-mm) seam allowance along either side from diagonal hem to bottom corners. Turn work wrong side out and stitch along seam again, leaving a ½-in (1.25-cm) seam allowance along the edge. Press seam to one side.

Now fold bottom edge 2 in (5 cm) over to the wrong side and press fold. Turn edge under again, pin in place, and topstitch hem. Repeat the process to hem unfinished edges at top of garment.

Attach a safety pin to one end of the silk ribbon and thread it through each of the hemmed sections at top of garment. Tie ends of strap into a bow at right and gather fabric toward the center.

HELPFUL HINT

While this gathered pattern has a very forgiving fit, it is important to be sure that you are purchasing fabrics that will work for your shape. Consider using lightweight fabrics such as cotton lawn, voile or silk charmeuse for a wonderful drape that will accentuate and flatter any figure without adding bulk.

wrap skirt

Flattering on any figure, this modern classic is elegant and versatile without being fussy. Tailored for you with just a few measurements and some basic math, you'll be amazed at how easy it is to make something so beautifully fitted.

PREPARATION

Begin by taking waist, hip, and length measurements for the skirt (see page 105). It is very important to measure yourself as accurately as possible. It is not the time to "suck it in." Instead, get comfortable with your curves and embrace your body type so that you can make a skirt perfectly fitted to your individual measurements.

First, measure around the narrowest part of your waist and write down this number (W). Next, measure and record your hip at the widest point (H). Figure the length of your skirt standing in front of a mirror. With good posture, hold the measuring tape at your waist and allow it to drape freely to the floor. Do not bend or stoop to read measurement, but instead use your reflection to make a note of the most flattering length (L).

Now that you have your measurements accurately recorded, a little math will help you complete your pattern.

Multiply waist measurement (W) by 1.5, then divide by 3 and add 1½ in (3.75 cm) for seam allowance. My waist is 31 in (79 cm), so 31 x 1.5 = 46½ (118.5 cm). Then 46½ ÷ 3 = 15½ + 1½ = 17 in (118.5 ÷ 3 = 39.5 + 3.75 = 43.25 cm) (A). Now repeat this formula with your hip measurements. My hip (H) measurement was 41 in (104 cm), so 41 x 1.5 = 61½ ÷ 3= 20½ + 1½ = 22 in (104 x 1.5 = 156 ÷ 3= 52 + 3.75 = 55.75 cm) (B). Add 2 in (5 cm)

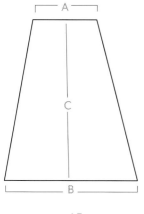

cut 3

to length (L) for hemming and seam allowance. My desired length was 30 in (76 cm), so 30 + 2 = 32 in (76 + 5 = 81 cm) (C). Following the diagram, measure and mark out pattern onto craft or pattern paper. If you have a bit more time or prefer a wider sash, measure and cut a panel 6 in (15 cm) x 4 times your waist measurement. If you prefer to skip this step, feel free to finish waist with bias tape instead.

Use your patterns to cut three skirt pieces and one sash panel from your fabric.

ASSEMBLY

Using French seaming method, align first skirt panel to second with wrong sides facing and stitch together ¼ in (6 mm) from edge. Press seam, fold panels so right sides are facing, and seam again ½ in (1.25 cm) from edge. Repeat to seam second skirt panel to third. Next, hem remaining cut edges by folding over ½ in (1.25 cm) twice. Pin, press, and topstitch.

Finally, with right sides facing, pin waistband into place along top edge of assembled skirt, and seam panels together. One side will need to wrap all the way around the body, so be sure to position piece off center, making one tie twice as long as the other. Press on right side, then fold belt to waistband with right sides facing. Stitch sash edges together on either side, leaving waistband open. Clip corners, turn belt and waistband right side out, and press seams flat. Fold, pin, and press sash panel into position at waist. Stitch seam closed.

shower cap

A purely practical shower cap is a thing of the past. Stitch one up with a bit of vintage vinyl and try it on for size. If you aren't really the shower cap type, use it in the kitchen instead as a lid to protect rising bread dough from drafts and dehydration.

PREPARATION

You will need to make a large circle template with a diameter of 20 in (55 cm). If you do not have a compass, draft this pattern using the string and pin method described below (see fig. 1). Use the template to cut one panel each from your fabric and vinyl pieces.

With a measuring tape, measure the circumference of your head. Trim the elastic to 2 in (5 cm) less than your head measurement.

string and pin method

Gently pin kitchen twine to center of paper. Attach pencil to a piece of twine 10 in (25 cm) from pin. With even tension on the twine, hold pencil perpendicular to the paper and rotate around pin marking a circle (see fig. 1). With craft scissors, trim out circle.

fig. 1

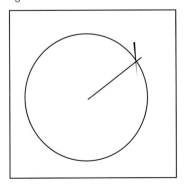

ASSEMBLY

With wrong sides facing, align fabrics and attach bias tape around the edge leaving a 2-in (5-cm) opening in the topstitching to insert elastic.

Attach safety pin to one end of the elastic and gently feed it into the bias tape trim. Pin free end of elastic to the outside of the trim so you don't lose it as you pull the elastic through. Feel for the safety pin and gently coax the elastic through the opening in the bias tape until it feeds out the other side. Check to be sure your elastic is not twisted, then stitch the ends together. Stitch opening in bias tape closed.

MATERIALS

⅔ yd (⅔ m) lightweight vinyl

⅔ yd (⅔ m) lightweight cotton or terry for lining (optional)

Thread to match vinyl

2 yds (2 m) bias tape to complement vinyl

⅔ yd (⅔ m) elastic ¼-in (6-mm) wide

EQUIPMENT

Large sheet of newspaper

Compass or ½ yd (½ m) kitchen twine

Ruler

Pen or pencil

Craft and fabric scissors

Straight pins

Measuring tape

Large safety pin

HELPFUL HINT

If you have never used bias tape, check out the Bias Binding tutorial on page 108.

hand warmers

Winter beckons with chilly fun with snowmen, igloos, and ice skating on the pond. Keep your little adventurer warm on winter expeditions and bus-stop mornings with these cozy microwaveable minis.

PREPARATION

Using the heart template on page 118, cut two pieces of fabric for each hand warmer. I suggest making at least two (one for each mitten).

ASSEMBLY

With right sides facing, stitch pieces together leaving 2-in (5-cm) opening to turn work. Clip corners and notch out curves. Turn work right side out and fill with flax seed. Stitch opening closed.

SEE TEMPLATE ON PAGE 118

MATERIALS

¼ yd (¼ m) medium-weight fabric

Thread to match fabric

Flax seed

EQUIPMENT

Tailor's chalk or transfer paper and tracing wheel

Fabric and craft scissors

HELPFUL HINT

Microwave heat varies greatly, so be sure to monitor heating times closely. Never leave items heating in the microwave unattended because, as with all microwavables, there is a potential for combustion if items are overheated. Recommended heating time is 15 seconds at lowest microwave setting. If more heat is desired, continue heating in 15-second increments, checking often until desired temperature is reached. Be sure to check temperature carefully before giving to children. Never allow children to heat items without adult supervision.

finger puppets

Need a distraction for rainy days or trips to the market? These adorable forest friends will have the kids inventing all kinds of adventures. This quick and easy finger puppet pattern will help you to create all five: Bunny, fox, bear, raccoon, and owl.

projects

PREPARATION

Using patterns provided on page 119, cut two main body shapes per puppet, and tail, ears, and eyes to match the animal you want to create as follows:

Bunny: Cut one nose panel, two ears and corresponding inserts (1A & 1B).
Fox: Cut two ears and inserts (3A & 3B), three tail tip/cheek fur panels (2B), and one tail piece (2A).
Bear: Cut two ears and inserts (4A & 4B), one nose, and one belly panel.
Raccoon: Cut two ears, one mask, one tail (2A), and three tail stripes.
Owl: Cut two ears, two wings, one beak, one belly, and one eye panel.

Don't be afraid to get creative to come up with your own unique combinations–remember strange little hybrids are especially compelling and most often possess a wild, wonderful magic all their own.

ASSEMBLY

Sew corresponding inserts onto ear and tail panels for following animals: Bunny (1A &1B), fox (2A & 2B and 3A & 3B), raccoon (2A & contrasting tail stripes), and bear (4A & 4B).

Place and stitch features onto front body panel as desired: Bunny

(apply nose panel), fox (2B—arrange triangular facial markings so tips meet at center nose area), raccoon (apply mask), bear (apply belly and nose panels), and owl (apply belly panel, stitch beak panel, and then apply eyes over beak panel).

If you are making an owl, attach wings to the back panel now. Position them so that when the body panels are joined the wings will be on the outside of the finger puppet.

Pin appropriate ear and tail pieces into place between body panels. Secure by topstitching around the edge of body panels, taking care to leave an opening at the bottom of the puppet for your finger.

With embroidery thread, stitch eyes and other facial features.

SEE TEMPLATES ON PAGE 119

MATERIALS

An assortment of felt sheets: dark brown, red brown, gray, tan, black, light green, and celadon

Contrasting or matching threads

Embroidery threads: black, pink, brown, and yellow

EQUIPMENT

Fabric scissors

Straight pins

Embroidery needle

SAVVY

flat doll dress up

Like paper dolls, these felted friends encourage imaginative play, which has been shown to positively impact early childhood learning and development. Interactive play helps to build social and cognitive skills, language, and narrative comprehension, as well as logical sequential thought and emotional impulse control. Sounds like fun...

doll

PREPARATION

The patterns provided on pages 120–123 are designed to be transferred onto felt and cut out. Use contrasting thread and follow the transferred lines—stitching by hand or with a machine— to create a "drawn" effect then trim away excess felt just outside of the lines. All wardrobe pieces are interchangeable so they can be used together in a variety of ways. Although it may take some time to get the hang of it, the fine stitch work will help to build your dexterity and sewing skill.

Begin by transferring and cutting out the paper templates for the doll silhouette, underwear, and accessories. Trace the outline of pattern pieces onto felt, and cut out. If you have difficulty transferring lines onto your felt, use your disappearing ink marker to retrace faint lines.

MATERIALS

Wool felt in a variety of colors

Sewing thread: contrasting and matching as desired

Embroidery thread in a variety of colors

½ yd (½ m) ½-in (1.25-cm) wide ribbon

Assortment of small buttons and embellishments for detailing accessories (optional)

EQUIPMENT

Transfer paper and tracing wheel

Disappearing ink marker

Craft, fabric and embroidery scissors

Hand-sewing needles

SAVVY

ASSEMBLY

Layer underwear panel over doll silhouette and topstitch around the outer edges of the underwear to secure. Embroider facial features onto doll if desired. With transfer paper and tracing wheel, transfer lines onto accessories and stitch using contrasting thread. Do not attach clothing, hair or accessories to the doll. These wardrobe pieces are meant to be mixed-and-matched to create a wide variety of characters and stories.

playhouse folio

PREPARATION

If you have a bit more time, make the playhouse folio for storage. Cut out four felt house panels (two interior and two exterior), two roof panels, six window squares, two doors, one dressing table, one pillow, and one blanket. Cut your ribbon in half.

ASSEMBLY

Stitch details onto each of the felt pieces before attaching to house panels. Stitch windows, roof, and door into place on the exterior house panels and set aside. Attach blanket and pillow to one of the interior panels, leaving one side of the pillow and the top of the blanket open for your storage compartments. On the other interior panel, attach the dressing table along three sides, leaving the top section open for additional storage.

Now that your house is appropriately decorated, place the two exterior panels side by side with right sides facing down. Place the interior scenes over the exterior panels so that edges align. Pin the ribbons between the panels at the center of the far left and far right sides. Pin the panels together, and stitch along the outer edges. Fold the joined panels so interiors are facing with ribbons together on one side. Pin along the edges to maintain alignment, and stitch together along the edge opposite the ribbons—your house should open and close like a book. Insert dolls and accessories, and tie closed with a pretty bow.

SEE TEMPLATES ON PAGES 120–123

> **HELPFUL HINT**
>
> Try out your darning or free-motion foot for the detailed line-work in this project, and don't forget to use your walking foot for thicker layers.

SAVVY

stuffed bunny

This little bunny is a sweet and gentle soul with a soft, fluffy tail. After an afternoon snack of alfalfa and clover, she loves to cuddle close to her favorite human for a quiet nap.

PREPARATION

Enlarge and cut out pattern pieces on page 123. For quicker layout and cutting, fold fabric in half then trace pattern pieces and cut through both layers. From main color fabric, you will need a total of four arm panels (makes two arms), two body panels, one back head panel, two ear panels, and one of each of the three face panels. Cut two more ear panels from the contrasting color fabric.

ASSEMBLY

First, make the ears. With right sides facing, align main and contrasting panels. Pin and stitch together around outer edge leaving straight edge at bottom open. Turn ears right side out, and press seams flat. Fold each ear in half with contrasting fabric on the inside, and baste along straight edge to maintain fold (see fig. 1).

Next, pin and stitch the three face panels together in order (see fig. 2). Pin ears to right side of assembled face panel so that the unfinished edges are at the top edge of the head, aligning the folds of the right and left ears with the right and left face seams (see fig. 3). Baste ears in place along the edge inside the ¼-in (6-mm) seam allowance. Fold ears over at the bottom front of work and pin together to keep them from being accidentally stitched into the seams in the next step. Place the back head panel on top of the assembled face panel, so that right sides are facing and outer edges are aligned. Stitch around outer edge leaving opening at the neck edge where ears protrude to turn work (see fig. 3).

Turn work right side out and embroider facial features: I used a satin stitch to create a triangle-shaped nose and French knots for eyes.

With right sides facing, stitch the body panels together leaving a 2-in (5-cm) opening at the top. Notch curves, especially around the seams at the underarms and between the legs. Turn work right side out. Stuff body to desired firmness and stitch opening closed. Repeat this process for each of the two arm pieces, seaming arm openings once stuffed.

Attach head to top of body and hand stitch into place using blind stitch. Pin arms in place on either side of the body. Place button on top of arm piece at the shoulder and stitch through the button and arm into main body, securing tightly with several stitches; tie a knot in your thread and pull it to the inside before cutting. Repeat process to attach the other arm to the other side of the body.

Make a small pom-pom (see page 113) and stitch to the back side. Tie ribbon at neck if desired.

SEE TEMPLATES ON PAGE 123

fig. 1

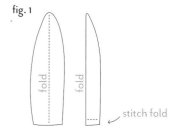

stitch fold

fig. 2

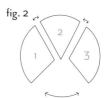

fig. 3

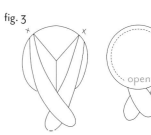

open

robot rattle

This darling robot wristlet entertains wee techies with his sweet jingle-jangle and an infectious smile. Tie the rattle to a car seat, stroller, or high chair, for a bit of fun-loving distraction that encourages independent play that boosts babies' brain development and motor skills.

PREPARATION

Cut two pieces of fabric 3 in x 3 in (7.5 cm x 7.5 cm). Using tracing wheel and transfer paper, transfer embroidery pattern for facial features onto the right side of one of the fabric panels, and embroider as desired.

ASSEMBLY

With right sides facing, place second panel on top of embroidered panel, and stitch panels together along outer edge leaving a 1-in (2.5-cm) opening to turn work. Trim corners and turn work right side out, using a point turner or knitting needle to gently push corners open, but take care not to press too hard or you will damage the seams. Stuff robot to half fullness and insert bell. Finish stuffing and stitch opening closed.

Fold ribbon in half and place fold at the center back of robot. Stitch ribbon securely into place. Tie ribbon around wrist, stroller, or other play space as desired.

SEE TEMPLATES ON PAGE 123

MATERIALS

Scrap of fabric measuring at least 3 in x 6 in (7.5 cm x 15 cm)

½ yd (½ m) ribbon

Small jingle bell

Sewing thread to match fabric

Embroidery threads

EQUIPMENT

Ruler or quilter's square

Fabric scissors

Point turner or knitting needle

Transfer paper and tracing wheel

Embroidery needle

HELPFUL HINT

Common sense dictates that babies and young children should never be left unattended. Be sure adult supervision is always provided when infants are playing with this or any other toy.

stroller cozy

Keep your little one warm and cozy all winter long with this comfy side-zip sleeper sack. This quilted blanket is customized to fit the strapping of your child's stroller, so it is sure to stay in place. Zip up for a snuggly day out, no matter the weather.

PREPARATION

From each of the main and coordinating fabrics, cut a panel measuring 48 in x 36 in (120 cm x 90 cm). Cut your batting panel to the same size. Sandwich batting between main and coordinating fabric panels with right sides out, then pin or baste layers together. Next, reference recommendations about design spacing on the batting packaging and use your tailor's chalk to mark out a simple straight stitch design onto the layered panel that is appropriate to these recommendations.

ASSEMBLY

Install your walking foot and quilt the panel using your marked design as a guide. Be sure to work systematically across the fabric panel, moving in the same direction with each pass, and beginning each stitch line at the same edge for best results.

Use a drinking glass to mark a curved edge at each corner, and trim any excess fabric for a pretty rounded edge. Apply bias tape along the edge of the panel.

Fold panel in half so it measures 36 in x 24 in (90 cm x 60 cm)—your main fabric should be visible on both sides of the fold with the coordinating fabric on the inside. Position sack in stroller and use tailor's chalk to mark the placement of openings for shoulder straps and buckles. As an example, the placement of my markings were as follows: Two vertical shoulder strap openings 6 in (15 cm) long placed 7 in (17.5 cm) from top, and 6½ in (16.5 cm) from the zipper edge, and 6½ in (16.5 cm) from the fold edge; one horizontal strap opening 2½ in (6.5 cm) wide centered 8 in (20 cm) below the vertical strap openings. Remember: Strollers have a wide variety of safety strap configurations so you

will need to measure the size and placement of the strapping for your individual stroller. Bind openings for strapping as you would a buttonhole (see the Buttons and Buttonholes tutorial on page 110).

Pin zipper into opening along the side of stroller sack so that bias edges meet at the center of zipper, and baste. Mark a stitch line ¼ in (6 mm) from the teeth along three sides of the zipper, leaving the top edge of zipper open. Install your zipper foot attachment and topstitch along the marked stitch line, pivoting at corners as detailed in the Zipper tutorial on page 113. Use blind stitch to stitch abutted bias edges closed at the bottom of the sack.

paper plane mobile

Childhood memories soar beyond the great blue yonder with this adorable mobile inspired by paper planes. A wonderful addition to any nursery or child's room, its gentle motion reminds us that adventures await as dreams take flight.

MATERIALS

5 x wool felt sheets 8 in x 12 in (20 cm x 30 cm)

½ yd (½ m) medium-weight cotton fabric

½ yd (½ m) cotton quilt batting

Wooden coat hanger

Threads to match fabric and felt

Embroidery thread or any heavyweight thread for stringing planes

EQUIPMENT

Craft and fabric scissors

Sheet of plain paper

Pencil or marker pen

Transfer paper and tracing wheel

Disappearing ink marker

Hand-sewing needle

HELPFUL HINT

When stringing your mobile, it may take a few tries to find the center point, which allows planes to hang in an evenly weighted position. Be patient. If you don't get it the first time around, remove the plane, and adjust your thread placement slightly until it is just right.

PREPARATION

Use the paper plane template on page 124 to mark 10–15 triangular plane panels onto your felt squares, using transfer paper and tracing wheel. (The number of planes and how you position them will add to the uniqueness of your mobile, so choose an amount that feels right to you.) Cut out the triangular panels. Fold each panel in half so that like sides match and press a crease at center along the fold. Stitch the folded panel together ¼ in (6 mm) from fold and press "wings" out to create plane shape. Firmly press together using steam. Repeat to make desired number of planes and set grouping aside. Trace the shape of your hanger onto a piece of plain paper. Next, calculate your seam allowance (C) by measuring the depth of your hanger (A) and adding it to your seam allowance (B). (Mine was ¼ in (6 mm) hanger depth (A) + ¼ in (6 mm) seam allowance (B) = ½ in (1.25 cm) added ease (C).) Add calculated seam allowance to the outside of your hanger outline, and cut out your pattern piece around the outer marked line. Using this template, mark and cut out two panels from fabric and two from batting.

ASSEMBLY

Place the two fabric panels together with right sides facing and edges aligned. Sandwich the fabric panels between the batting panels and pin all four layers together. Now, stitch panels together along both sides, leaving bottom edge open and just enough space at the top to insert coat hanger without allowing unfinished edges to poke through. Turn work right side out and slip over the hanger. Stitch the bottom seam closed using blind stitch (see fig. 1).

Cut three or four lengths of thread 24–36 in (60–90 cm). With a hand-sewing needle, string planes through center fold at desired spacing.

SEE TEMPLATE ON PAGE 124

fig.1

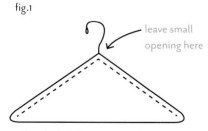

leave small opening here

hand stitch here once in place

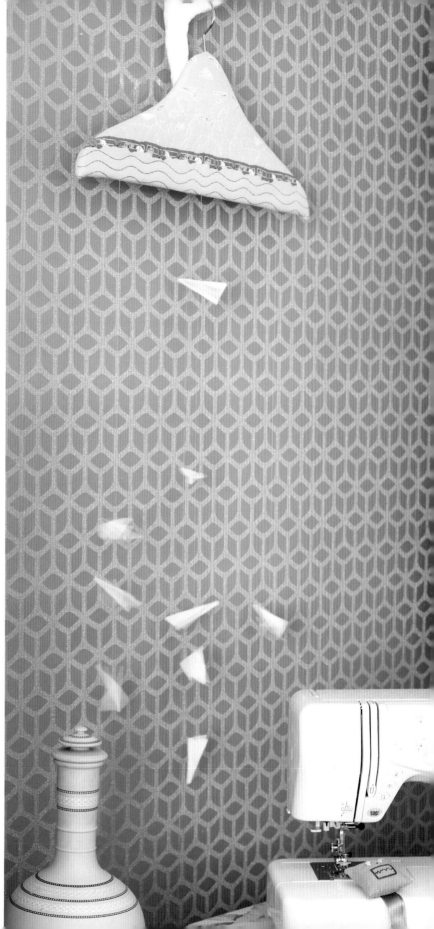

fingerless gloves

Technophiles and tree huggers alike will love these fashion-forward fingerless gloves. Retired woolens are cleverly recycled into a knitwear design that allows for dexterity and texting on the go.

PREPARATION

Begin by taking overall measurements of your hands. Firstly, measure the circumference of your hand at the widest point over your thumb for the width (A). Next, calculate the length of your mittens by measuring from the wrist to the second knuckle of the middle finger (B), then add 2–3 in (5–7.5 cm) for cuff, depending on your preferred length, to give you the height (C)—see fig. 1. Use these calculated measurements to mark out and cut two rectangular pieces from the felted wool. Your panels should measure A x C (width x height).

Now calculate the sizing for your thumb cutout. Measure from the center knuckle of your forefinger to the crease between first finger and thumb (D). Now measure the circumference of your thumb (E). Add ½ in (1.25 cm) to each of these measurements for your calculated thumb gusset measurements: D + ½ in (1.25 cm) = F and E + ½ in (1.25 cm) = G. At the top center point of each of the felted wool panels, measure and mark a rectangle that measures G x F (width x height), then cut this smaller rectangular section away (see fig. 2).

ASSEMBLY

With right sides facing, fold panel in half and stitch the seam above thumb opening together with a ¼-in (6-mm) seam allowance. Apply bias tape or a piece of ½-in (1.25-cm) knit ribbing along the top edge and around the thumb opening for finishing if desired. Be sure to cut ribbing ½ in (1.25 cm) longer than the edge to which you will apply it. Maintain your ¼-in (6-mm) seam allowance.

Apply bias tape to each edge of the side seam. Measure and mark out openings for ribbon lacing. Stitch buttonholes or fix grommets into fabric at marked points (see fig. 3). Thread ribbon through buttonholes/grommets in a criss-cross fashion as you would shoe laces, and tie at the wrist.

MATERIALS

Recycled felted wool sweaters

Thread to match

Bias tape (optional)

Grommets (optional)

3 yds (3 m) ½-in (1.25-cm) wide silk ribbon

EQUIPMENT

Tailor's chalk

Fabric scissors or pinking shears

Straight pins

Grommet tool (optional)

HELPFUL HINT

For a fitted look utilize the sleeves and cuffs of your recycled felted wool sweaters for gathering at the wrist.

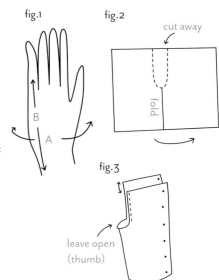

fig.1

fig.2

cut away

fold

B

A

fig.3

leave open (thumb)

silhouette applique

Recall days past with this charming Victorian keepsake and make memories that will last a lifetime. Collaborate with children or loved ones and capture their likenesses to create tiny works of art that will be cherished for generations to come.

PREPARATION

Have your child stand against a white or light colored wall and photograph them in profile. Make a 5 in x 7 in (13 cm x 18 cm) print of your photo. You can use an inexpensive plain paper for this part of the process because you will be cutting the image out to use as a template of your child's silhouette, but first trace the outer edge of your child's profile with a pen or pencil to accentuate the outline. Cut out the shape along this outline.

Pin your silhouette template to the felt. Use tailor's chalk to trace the outline, then cut it out. Cut background fabric to fit frame (mine was 5 in x 7 in/13 cm x 18 cm).

ASSEMBLY

Place felt panel at center of background fabric and pin in place. Attach silhouette to background using a chain stitch, or other decorative stitch, along outer edge. Frame and hang as desired.

HELPFUL HINT

If you have a bit more time, consider adding some information about your loved one before framing: Embroider the date, their name, age, and why they are special to you.

SAVVY

tailor's ham and sleeve roll

There are many sizes and uses for a tailor's ham and sleeve roll. Sized for easy storage, these patterns serve a wide range of pressing possibilities. They are well-suited to the needs of most home tailors. As your skills progress, consider adjusting the basic templates to suit your preferences.

PREPARATION

Use the tailor's ham template on page 124 to cut one panel from wool fabric, one panel from heavyweight cotton or duck cloth, and two panels from cotton batting.

ASSEMBLY

Place the wool and cotton fabric panels together with right sides facing, and sandwich between the two batting panels. Align panels and pin along the edges. Stitch panels together along the outside edge leaving a 2–3 in (5–7.5 cm) opening along the bottom edge for stuffing. Notch and trim panels along curved edges. If you are unfamiliar with notching, check out the tutorial in the

Techniques and Skill Builders section on page 109.

To turn work right side out, insert your hand between the wool and cotton fabrics to grasp the furthest edge and pull it through the opening to the outside. Use the handle of the wooden spoon to gently smooth interior seam edges.

Begin packing your ham firmly with stuffing or flax seed. Use your spoon to compact stuffing tightly as you go. The surface area of your ham should be extremely firm—almost hard—when complete, so try to "over-stuff" it. Hand-stitch opening closed with blind stitch.

Repeat this process to make a sleeve roll using the sleeve roll template on page 124.

SEE TEMPLATES ON PAGE 124

MATERIALS

¼ yd (¼ m) wool felt or heavyweight wool coating material

¼ yd (¼ m) medium-weight to heavyweight cotton fabric or duck cloth

¼ yd (¼ m) cotton batting

Thread to match fabrics

Sawdust or flax seed

EQUIPMENT

Transfer paper and tracing wheel

Craft and fabric scissors

Straight pins

Wooden spoon

Hand-sewing needle

HELPFUL HINT

To ensure a solid pressing tool that is properly weighted, be sure to stuff your tailor's ham or sleeve roll with one of the suggested materials rather than a typical stuffing material. Another alternative is pet bedding with fine shredded chips.

SAVVY

change purse

Tired of digging through your bag or pockets for coins at the newsstand, laundromat, and gumball machine? Look no further than this trusty change purse to keep all that spare change squared away—if you carry one of these you'll be well-stocked at wishing wells and will always have your two cents ready.

PREPARATION

Using transfer paper and tracing wheel, transfer templates onto a piece of paper and cut out. Trace transferred shapes onto wrong side of felt or leather. Cut material ¼ in (6 mm) outside of marked lines. For a decorative edge, consider using pinking shears when cutting out panels (be sure to match edges).

ASSEMBLY

Place smaller panel on top of the larger panel so that the curvature is aligned, and topstitch ⅛ in (3 mm) from outside edge. You may want to consider using a walking foot when stitching through thicker fabrics, and if your choice of material is leather, be sure to use a leather needle to ensure good stitch quality.

Attach a small button into place at top center of smaller panel. Cut a small buttonhole opening at top center of larger panel in line with the button placement.

SEE TEMPLATES ON PAGE 125

MATERIALS
⅛ yd (⅛ m) felt or leather

Heavy-duty thread

Small button

EQUIPMENT
Transfer paper and tracing wheel

Craft scissors

Fabric scissors or pinking shears

Tailor's chalk or disappearing ink marker

Leather sewing machine needle

HELPFUL HINT
It may only be possible to buy leather as a whole hide, so when shopping ask for remnants or bolt ends as an alternative. Because leather stretches with use, it is a good idea to cut your buttonhole a bit smaller than the button that will be used.

SAVVY

phone wallet

With just enough space for the essentials, this little dynamo will keep you organized on the go. Stash your cell phone, a credit card, lipstick, and keys then head out for a bit of unfettered fun.

PREPARATION

Determine the size of your cell phone and add 1½ in (3.75 cm) to the overall dimensions: Measured height + 1½ in (3.75 cm) = HEIGHT and measured width + 1½ in (3.75 cm) = WIDTH. Using your quilter's square, measure and mark out a rectangle onto a sheet of plain paper with the calculated height and width measurements, then cut out your pattern template using craft scissors.

Fold fabric in half with right sides facing, then fold in half again, and trace the outline of your pattern template onto the top layer of fabric. With sharp fabric scissors, cut through all four layers of fabric and set aside.

Take your pattern template and make a mark ½ in (1.25 cm) from one end along one of the long sides. Next, measure and mark the center point of the other long side. Now draw a diagonal line from this center point to the first mark made. With craft scissors, cut your template in two along this line and use the larger piece to mark a pocket panel on the wrong side of your fabric. Cut one pocket panel.

ASSEMBLY

Apply bias to angled edge of pocket panel. If you have never used bias tape before, check out the tutorial in the Techniques and Skill Builders section on page 108.

Place pocket panel on top of one of the set aside rectangular fabric panels so that right sides of both panels are visible, and baste the pocket into place. Now orient your panel so that the widest edge of the pocket is at the bottom and mark the top edge with a pin for reference. Place another rectangular panel over the pocketed panel and baste the two together along the pin-marked edge. Run a line of reinforcement stitches ½-in (1.25-cm) long at each end of the basted seam. Press seams open.

MATERIALS

¼ yd (¼ m) medium-weight to heavyweight cotton fabric

¼ yd (¼ m) cotton batting

¼ yd (¼ m) ½-in (1.25-cm) wide double fold bias tape

9 in (22.5 cm) zipper to match fabric

Thread to match fabric

EQUIPMENT

Quilter's square

Plain paper

Pencil

Tailor's chalk or disappearing ink marker

Craft and fabric scissors

Zipper foot

Hand-sewing needle

SAVVY

Center zipper on the seam just stitched and baste it into place. If your zipper is a bit long, shorten it by zigzagging a line of stitches across the zipper at the point you would like the opening to end. Measure and mark a line ¼ in (6 mm) on either side of the zipper seam using a disappearing ink marker or a new piece of tailor's chalk. Attach zipper foot to your machine and stitch the zipper into place along your markings. You can do this with a single line of stitches, by ending each line with your needle in the down position: Lift your presser foot and pivot your panel 90 degrees so that

your foot is aligned with the next line, then lower presser foot and continue stitching. If you are new to zippers, review the tutorial in the Techniques and Skill Builders section on page 113.

Once you have installed your zipper, remove basting stitches and check the functionality of your zipper. It should open and close easily. Next, fold panel in half along zipper edge with right sides facing and pin seams together along unfinished edges. Sew seams together with a ½-in (1.25-cm) seam allowance and turn work right side out.

To make the lining, align the two remaining rectangular panels so right sides are facing, and stitch together along three sides leaving one of the long sides open. Fold over unfinished edges at the opening by ½ in (1.25 cm) and press a crease into the fold. Place lining panel inside zippered pouch and, with open edge aligned to zipper edge, stitch into place along either side of the zipper.

lunch sack

Send them back to school with a smile and encourage healthy eating habits all year long. This insulated bag and optional cooling square will keep mid-day meals properly chilled until the lunch bell rings.

PREPARATION

With quilter's square, measure and mark out a rectangle 30 in x 13½ in (75 cm x 33.75 cm). Cut panel out using pinking shears for a cute finished edge.

ASSEMBLY

With right sides facing, fold fabric in half and stitch seams together at either side with a ¼-in (6-mm) seam allowance. Rotate piece so one of your side seams is centered and aligned with the seam at the back (see fig. 1). Use your hands to press panel flat so that the lower corner comes to a peak. Using your quilter's square, measure 2 in (5 cm) up from the point and draw a line perpendicular to the seam. Stitch along this line and trim away excess fabric. Repeat on the back seam. Turn work right side out.

Fold elastic in half and pin cut edges together to form a loop. Center folded elastic at the top edge of one side of your bag. Stitch piece into place so the loop extends out from the edge. On the other side of the bag, attach the button 6 in (15 cm) below the top edge at center.

OPTIONAL ADD-ONS

For added insulation, cut two additional pattern pieces (30 in x 13 ½ in/75 cm x 33.75 cm)—one from thermal batting and one from lining fabric. Follow assembly instructions for the outer bag above. Do not turn work right side out. Insert insulated layer into outer bag, then insert the lining. Fold layers over ½ in (1.25 cm) to the wrong side so that the unfinished edges are concealed. Topstitch along fold securing it just below the pinked edge of the outer bag.

To make a cooling square, cut two panels 8½ in x 4½ in (21.25 cm x 11.25 cm). With right sides facing, stitch around edge leaving a 2-in (5-cm) opening on one side. Trim corners and turn work right side out. Fill with flax seed to about half fullness and stitch opening closed. Place cooled pack in the bottom of lunch sack and roll up bag to retain the chill.

MATERIALS

½ yd (½ m) laminated fabric or oilcloth

Thread to match fabric

1½ in (3.75 cm) thin elastic or elastic cord

½ in (1.25 cm) button

½ yd (½ m) thermal batting and lining fabric (optional)

Flax seed (optional)

EQUIPMENT

Quilter's square

Disappearing ink marker or tailor's chalk

Pinking shears

Fabric scissors

Hand-sewing needle

HELPFUL HINT

Store your cooling square in the freezer inside a zip-top plastic bag to prevent odor absorption and keep it super cool.

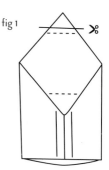

fig 1

SAVVY

casserole carrier

Picnic or potluck—you'll be the life of the party with this clever casserole carrier. Transport hot dishes without burning yourself and keep food warm until it's time to serve. Whip one up for the hostess of the next Supper Club or say "Thank You" to your favorite foodie.

PREPARATION

Measure, mark, and cut fabrics and batting to 30 in x 37 in (75 cm x 92.5 cm). Lay out each fabric panel with right sides facing and fold in quarters (fold in half and then fold in half again along the other edge). Your panel should be almost square with all four corners stacked in alignment.

Measure and mark out another smaller rectangle 10½ in x 8 in (26.5 cm x 20 cm) on the folded fabric panels along the edges where all four corners meet. With fabric scissors, cut away smaller rectangle and unfold panels. You should now have what resembles a plus sign. Now center a saucer along each of the two wider (15-in/37.5-cm) edges and mark out matching crescents on each

side of panel. Trim along curved lines, and remove the curved sections. Place fabrics on top of batting so edges are aligned, then mark and cut out the shaping. Pin layers together.

ASSEMBLY

Starting at the center of one of the non-crescent edges, stitch the panels together along edges with a ½-in (1.25-cm) seam allowance, leaving a 4-in (10-cm) opening to turn work. Notch out corners and curves with a pair of sharp fabric scissors. Now turn your work right side out by reaching between the two fabric panels and pulling right side through opening. You may find it helpful to use a point turner or knitting needle to press corners open. Do not poke too hard. Press along seams. Stitch opening closed and topstitch along the edges if desired. On the crescent edge, fold edge over dowel so that it is snuggly fitted and the dowel is exposed at center. Pin fold over and stitch in place. Repeat on other side.

Place casserole dish at the center of carrier and fold straight-edged panels to center so that they overlap firmly (see fig. 1). Mark the point of overlap on each side with a pin or two. Cut a 2½-in (6.25-cm) piece of Velcro, separate the two parts, and

attach on either side of the carrier at the marked points. When overlapped, the Velcro strips should align and lock in place to hold inner panels together snuggly. Add another section of Velcro to the handled section just below the cutouts if desired.

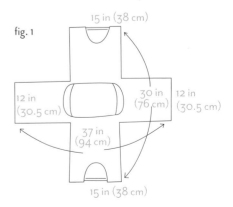

fig. 1

15 in (38 cm)

12 in (30.5 cm)

30 in (76 cm)

12 in (30.5 cm)

37 in (94 cm)

15 in (38 cm)

bike basket

Ding...ding...ding! Few things dress up a bike like the flirty functionality of a basket. Recycled denim and waistband handles add sustainability and durability to this convertible carry-all. Then simply detach your basket and the tiny tote does double duty.

PREPARATION

Using pattern on page 125, cut two base panels, one from main fabric and one from lining fabric. Measure and cut two side panels 7½ in x 31½ in (18.75 cm x 78.75 cm), one from main fabric and one from lining fabric. From main fabric, measure and cut four handle panels 2 in x 13 in (5 cm x 32.5 cm) each. To give added structure, measure and cut one piece of aluminum screening 7½ in x 31½ in (18.75 cm x 78.75 cm) if desired.

ASSEMBLY

With right sides facing, match side and base panels of main fabric and pin together so that the longer edge of the rectangular side panel aligns with the outer edge of the oval base panel. Stitch panels together maintaining a ½-in (1.25-cm) seam allowance. Continuing to work with right sides facing, pin short edges of rectangular side panel together where they meet and stitch seam together. This is the basic shape of the basket. Repeat this process for the fabric lining.

Next, turn main fabric "basket" right side out and insert the lining piece into it so that shape and edges are aligned. The right sides of each panel should be visible, interior and exterior, and the unfinished edges on the bottom edge should be concealed inside of the basket. Check your alignment to be sure that seams and edges are perfectly aligned. If you maintained a consistent seam allowance while stitching pieces together, you should be ready for the next step. If you find any discrepancies, correct them and re-stitch seams as needed.

Insert screen panel between interior and exterior panels to add structure and durability to shape. You may want to fold screening over slightly to prevent sharp edges from poking through seams later on.

With right sides facing, stitch two of the handle panels together at long edges. Turn work right side out and topstitch either side. Repeat to make second handle. Cut your length of ribbon/Velcro in half. Fold each of the cut pieces in half and stitch to the back side of each of the handle straps, so that the fold aligns with the unfinished edge. Fold interior and exterior side panels to wrong side and insert handles between layers so they are evenly spaced on either side, and pin in place. Topstitch layers together. Attach basket to the handlebars.

SEE TEMPLATE ON PAGE 125

SAVVY

book cover

In a digital age it's nice to have a place to make a note or two. Whether recording personal thoughts and daily to-dos or jotting phone messages, grocery lists, and important mustn't forgets, this practical pocketed organizer keeps everything conveniently at hand and in its place.

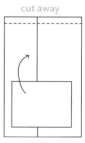

PREPARATION

With book closed, use your measuring tape to measure book height and girth. The girth is the width + depth, so measure from front right edge across the spine all the way to the back left edge. My book measured 8¼ in x 13¼ in (20.5 cm x 33.25 cm), and my calculations will help you to double-check measurements for the fit of your book as you go along. Before beginning layout, check that your fabric and grain are square.

On a flat surface, lay out main fabric so the wrong side is facing up and selvedge is at the top. Fold fabric in half so selvedges meet at the top. Now fold left edge over 4 in (10 cm). Press and pin folded (pocket) section through layers (see fig. 1).

Place bottom edge of book ⅛ in (3 mm) from the pressed edge (spine should be oriented along the bottom fold of fabric). With a pin, mark ⅛ in (3 mm) above the top edge of the book. Now, maintaining orientation, gently slide book to selvedge edge and repeat measurement. You have just added ease, which will allow your book to slip into the cover more easily once everything is stitched up. Fold fabric over at pins and press (this pressed line will be a guide for stitching later). Working out from the line you just pressed, measure another ½ in (1.25 cm) for seam allowance. Mark and cut fabric along this line (see fig. 2).

Next, you will need to figure out the measurements for your inner flap panels. Since the width of these is fairly standard, record this dimension

fig.1

fold

4 in (10cm)

fig.2

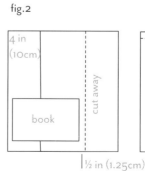

4 in (10cm)

book

cut away

cut away

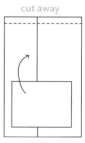

½ in (1.25cm)

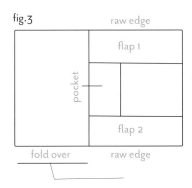

fig.3

raw edge

flap 1

pocket

flap 2

fold over   raw edge

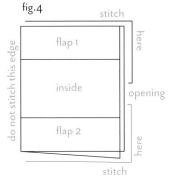

fig.4

stitch

do not stitch this edge

flap 1

inside

flap 2

stitch here

opening

stitch here

stitch

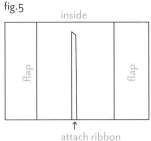

fig.5

inside

flap

flap

↑
attach ribbon

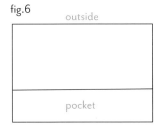

fig.6

outside

pocket

as 7 in (17.5 cm). Now figure the height measurements as follows: Height of book + ½ in (1.25 cm) for seam allowance = panel height. I calculated the flap height for my book as 8¼ in + ½ in = 8¾ in (20.5 cm + 1.25 cm = 21.75 cm). My panel dimensions were 8¾ in x 7 in (20.5 in x 17.5 in). Measure and cut two inner flap panels.

ASSEMBLY

With right sides facing, fold inner flap panel in half vertically (3.5 in/ 8.75 cm x calculated height). Stitch seams together along each of the shorter sides. Turn work right side out and press. Repeat for second panel.

Fold out bottom layer of fabric (the pocket and top layer are pinned together). Pin flap panels into place over pocket on either side of cover so raw edges match up. Baste flaps into place along either edge (see fig. 3).

Fold bottom layer over the top of work so the edges of cover align (the flaps are now inside) and pin in place. Stitch along the edge of each of the flaps leaving an opening between the flaps at the top of the cover to turn your work (see fig. 4). Clip corners and turn work right side out. Press seams flat. To add an optional bookmark: Fold ribbon in half, insert

fold into center opening, and stitch closed (see fig. 5).

If everything went as planned, your flaps should still be unattached at the bottom, which will enable you to stitch sections into the front pocket more easily. Start by pinning your ribbon and flaps safely out of the pocket area to avoid stitching them into a pocket seam. Working on the outside of the cover (fig. 6), mark out pocket sections as desired with a ruler and disappearing ink marker: pencil pockets are usually about 1 in (2.5 cm) each, and I made one pocket large enough to accommodate a calculator or cell phone. Just remember to consider the object's girth when measuring and add a bit of ease for best fit. Stitch along marked lines, reinforcing openings with a few backstitches for strength.

kimono blouse

The effortlessness of a traditional kimono lends its ageless simplicity to this quick blouse. Choose lightweight silks or voiles for elegant eveningwear, or a weightier woven fabric for everyday wearability.

PREPARATION

Begin by taking the following torso measurements:
A: Length—shoulder to hip
B: Hip/Bust—record your measurements at the widest part of your bust and hip
C: Shoulder to shoulder
D: Top shoulder seam to wrist with arm straight down

Refer to the Taking Measurements tutorial on page 105 for a refresher on accurately establishing your measurements.
For my kimono blouse, I determined my measurements to be as follows:
A: 20 in (50 cm)
B: 44 in/38 in (110 cm /95 cm)
C: 16 in (40 cm)
D: 20 in (50 cm)

To customize fit to your size, add 10 in (25 cm) to hip (or bust measurement if larger) then divide in half for overlap. In my case, 54 in ÷ 2 = 27 in (137 cm ÷ 2 = 68.5 cm), so 27 in (68.5 cm) is the amount of overlap I'll need to take into consideration when cutting the pattern.

Now that you have your measurements, proceed by folding fabric in half with right sides facing and selvedges together. Mark center line. Measure 11 in (27.5 cm) below the fold and draw a line parallel to the fold across work. Using the marked line at center front as your mid-point, draw two lines (one on either side of center line) using your calculated hip measurement. Start at the fold and continue marking across work parallel to the center line to the selvedge edge. For my kimono blouse, I measured 27 in (68.5 cm) from the center mark on either side and used my quilter's square to draw the lines. Congratulations – you have created the basic outline of your blouse.

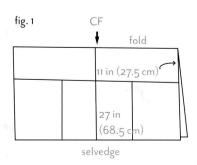

fig. 1
CF
fold
11 in (27.5 cm)
27 in (68.5 cm)
selvedge

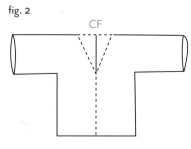

fig. 2
CF

ASSEMBLY

Next, cutaway the rectangular areas created at the bottom left and bottom right, cutting through both layers to leave a "T" shape (fig. 1). What will eventually become the neck and sleeves extends across the fabric along the fold with the body of the blouse below, which is the width of your widest measurement plus 10 in (25 cm).

For the neckline, mark 4 in (10 cm) on either side of center point. Then measure 8 in (20 cm) from fold and mark. Draw two lines to connect the 4-in (10-cm) marks to the 8-in (20-cm) mark, creating a "V" shape (see fig. 2). Cutting only through the top layer of fabric, cut along the center line, then trim along diagonals and across fold, to make an opening along the fold.

Seam along the underarms from sleeves to hip. To turn work at armpit, end sewing with the needle in down position, lift foot and pivot work 90 degrees, lower foot and continue to edge. Notch out the corner (see the Notching, Clipping and Curves tutorial, page 109). You can trim seams with pinking shears to prevent fraying, or apply bias tape for a couture finish. Apply bias tape around front opening and neck. Hem sleeves and unfinished edge at the hip.

men's tie

Boring clichés are thoughtfully reinvented with this modern remake of a classic gift for dad—they're sure to appreciate the indulgent luxury of a bespoke tie.

PREPARATION

Several pattern templates will need to be drafted and cut out before you begin. Note that all pattern pieces are laid out and cut on the bias (at a 45-degree angle to the fabric grain). If you have never worked on the bias, check out the tutorial on page 108.

You will need to measure and cut out one interfacing panel, one tie panel from your main fabric, and two lining fabric panels. The lining fabrics can be cut from the main fabric, or you can use an additional coordinating fabric.

Refer to the interfacing template diagram on page 93 (fig. 1), and begin drafting measurements directly onto interfacing. First, mark out and draw center line A to a length of 58 in (147 cm). Using your quilter's square, three additional lines will be made perpendicular along line A as follows:

Measure and mark line B at 2 in (5cm) in from one end of line A. Center and extend this mark 2 in (5cm) above the initial line A and 2 in (5cm) below for a total length of 4 in (10 cm). Measure and mark line C parallel to line B at 1 in (2.5 cm) in from the other end of line A. Now extend this line to ¾ in (2 cm) on either side of line A—a total length of 1½ in (4 cm).

Measure 28 in (70 cm) from line C and make line D parallel to line C and of equal length—¾ in (1.9 cm) on either side of line A. For reference, line D will be 25 in (63.5 cm) in from line

B. You should now have three lines running perpendicular to the first.

With a yardstick or quilter's square, connect the outermost points of the previously drafted lines to create the outline of your tie interfacing panel. Work across the top of your pattern, connecting the end of line A to the

MATERIALS

1¼ yds (1¼ m) 60-in (150-cm) wide lightweight to medium-weight fabric such as cotton lawn or silk shantung

¼ yd (¼ m) lightweight to medium-weight coordinating fabric for lining (optional)

1⅔ yds (1⅔ m) medium-weight to heavyweight sew-in interfacing

Small length of ¼–½-in (0.75–1.25-cm) wide ribbon for keeper

Thread to match fabric

EQUIPMENT

Yardstick or quilter's square

Marker pen

Craft and fabric scissors

Straight pins

Hand-sewing needle

Point turner or knitting needle

Transfer paper and smooth tracing wheel (optional)

top point of line C, connect line C to line D, and finally connect line D to the other end of line B. Repeat along the bottom edge connecting line A to the bottom edge of line B. In turn connect line B to D, line D to C, and line C to A, closing the loop. Cut interfacing along the outer lines you just drew. If you think you may want

fig.1

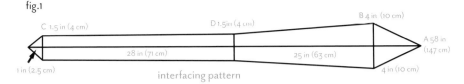

C 1.5 in (4 cm)   D 1.5in (4 cm)   B 4 in (10 cm)

A 58 in (147 cm)

28 in (71 cm)   25 in (63 cm)

1 in (2.5 cm)   4 in (10 cm)

interfacing pattern

fig.2

C 3.25 in (8 cm)   D 3.25 in (8 cm)   B 9.5 in (24 cm)

25 in (63.5 cm)   4.5 in (11.5 cm)   A 59 in (150 cm)

28 in (71 cm)

1.5 in (4 cm)

tie pattern

fig.3   lining A pattern

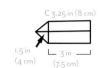

C 3.25 in (8 cm)

1.5 in (4 cm)   3 in (7.5 cm)

fig.4   lining B pattern

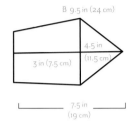

B 9.5 in (24 cm)

4.5 in (11.5 cm)

3 in (7.5 cm)

7.5 in (19 cm)

to make more ties at a later date, you can trace this interfacing panel onto a large sheet of paper and label it.

Using the measurements and diagrams as a guide, repeat this process on paper to create templates for the tie pattern (fig. 2) and corresponding lining pieces (figs. 3 and 4), keeping in mind that these pieces are larger than the interfacing. The lining pattern pieces are shaped to match the ends of your tie. To save time, fold your tie pattern at the appropriate points and retrace the shortened sections onto another sheet of paper, rather than redrafting these sections.

Using your craft scissors, cut out paper patterns for the tie and lining. With the wrong side of fabric facing up, layout pattern pieces on the bias and cut out tie and lining panels.

ASSEMBLY

Place tie panel right side down on a smooth, flat surface. Without stretching the piece out of shape, be sure your panel is as straight as possible, and smooth any edges that are out of place. Place the interfacing on top of the tie panel (wrong side is up), so that the center of each piece is aligned with the other. You may want to hand baste the two panels together along the center line for ease of handling as you turn work.

Turn tie panel over so right side is facing up, align lining panel B to corresponding section of tie so that right sides are facing. Pin layers together just where the point will form at the seam allowance. You can easily find this point by folding your panels along the center line and placing the pin ½ in (1.25 cm) from the point along the center line. With a needle and thread, tack this point in place with a few small stitches (also known as stay stitching). Stitching the tie in this way will help to stabilize the fabric and give a nice clean point when you turn your work.

Stitch the lining fabric to the main fabric along either edge. Trim your point just a little above the stay stitches and turn work right side out. Use a point turner or knitting needle to gently ease the point into place if needed but take care not to stretch or press it out of shape. Press seams flat and repeat process at other end of tie for lining panel A.

Once you have attached and pressed linings at either end, place your tie in a straight line on a flat surface, linings facing up. Fold over, pin and press remaining edges by

½ in (1.25 cm) for an even seam allowance all the way around. Next, fold your tie in thirds so the side seams overlap slightly at the center back side of the tie, and pin the seam into place as you work. Using blind stitch, hand sew this seam together. Add extra stay stitching at the beginning and end of the seam for a sturdier finish. Remove basting stitches.

SAVVY

weekend bag

Nothing beats a weekend away—it's time to relax and recharge. This oversized satchel is large enough to stow a few extras just in case you decide to stay an extra day or two.

PREPARATION

Seam allowances for this project are ½ in (1.25 cm) unless otherwise stated. If you are finishing the interior with bias tape, apply it to the seams as you are assembling the pieces. If you do not wish to bind your seams with bias tape, consider cutting out your pieces with pinking shears to prevent excessive fraying.

Measure and cut the following pieces from your fabric: Two zipper panels 36 in x 7 in (90 cm x 18 cm), one bottom panel 13 in x 38 in (33 cm x 95 cm), two side panels 16 in x 21 in (40.5 cm x 55 cm). Use the edge of a dinner plate to mark a curved edge on the upper left and right corners of the side panels. Trim away corners. Cut one outer pocket panel (optional) 10 in x 21 in (25 cm x 55 cm). If you are adding the outer pocket, apply bias tape to the top edge, then baste it into place along the sides and bottom edge of one of the side panels.

ASSEMBLY

Begin by installing zipper centered along the 36-in (90-cm) edge of the zipper panels. If installing a zipper is new to you, check out the tutorial in the Techniques and Skill Builders section on page 113.

Once your zipper is installed, press panel flat to smooth folded edge and create crisp edge along zipper opening. Place the zippered panel face down on the bottom panel (13 in x 38 in/33 cm x 95 cm) so that right sides are facing and shorter edges are matched. Pin along one of the shorter edges and stitch together.

Next, with right sides facing, center and pin the zippered panel along the top curved edge of the first of the side panels. Continue pinning the panel into place all along the outer edge of side panel until the short edges meet on the other side (fig. 1). Stitch this seam and repeat process on the other side with second side panel. Once the sides are installed, pin remaining opening and stitch seam closed.

Turn bag right side out. Remove any basting stitches that may be showing at the seams. Center and attach leather-strap handles on either side of the bag (fig. 2).

MATERIALS

1¼–1¾ yds (1¼–1¾ m) heavyweight canvas or upholstery fabric

36-in (90 cm) metal zipper

2 x 28-in (71-cm) leather straps

Thread to match fabric

4 yds (4 m) bias tape (optional)

EQUIPMENT

Fabric scissors or pinking shears

Dinner plate

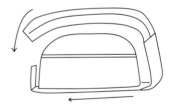

fig.1

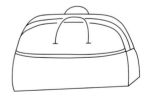

fig.2

slippers

A pair of shoes, a bit of fabric and a notion or two is all that you will need to create this customized slipper set. Whip up a pair for that special someone, or treat yourself and banish the barefoot blues all season long.

PREPARATION

Begin by tracing the soles of a pair of snuggly fitting shoes onto the plastic quilting template material. With craft scissors, trim out pattern pieces along marked outline. Fold fabric in half so that right sides are facing, then position left and right templates so that grain is centered along the length of the soles. Double-check the direction of your fabric pattern. Is the print orientation consistent for right and left slippers? Trace plastic template pattern onto fabric using a disappearing ink marker. Measure and mark a second line (for seam allowance) ½ in (1.25 cm) outside the template pattern lines, then carefully cut through both layers of the folded fabric along the outside line.

You now have four sole panels (two for the left and two for the right). To avoid confusion, I recommend orienting the pair and pinning a piece of paper with the markings "left" and "right" to the top of each corresponding foot bed before you set these panels aside. It is very easy to mistake the orientation and to end up with "two left feet," so this additional step will be well worth the effort. Repeat process to create four matching batting panels.

To determine your strap sizing, measure across the top of your shoe at the widest point (this should be back from the toe but forward from the instep). Be sure to measure all the way across from one side of the sole to the other. Now mark out and cut four rectangular strap panels (two each for left and right straps). These should measure 4 in (10 cm) x your width measurement. My width measurement was 8 in (20 cm), so my panels were cut 4 in x 8 in (10 cm x 20 cm). Repeat process to create four matching batting panels.

ASSEMBLY

assemble the straps

Arrange strap panels with right sides facing and directionality matched. If you are adding the optional piping, be sure to pin it in place along the longer edges between your main fabric panels now (see Helpful Hint). Place this configuration on top of two layers of batting and pin in place. Stitch all four layers together along the longer edges on either side of the panels. Be sure to leave shorter ends unstitched so that you can turn work right side out. To turn work, reach between fabric layers and gently pull furthest edge through the opening so that main fabrics are facing out on either side. Press flat along seams. Repeat process for second strap.

attach strap to slipper sole

With right sides facing up, pin strap into place so that it is centered at the widest point (between toe and instep) of the left top sole panel. Baste strap into place on either side of sole ¼ in (6 mm) from the edge. Now place the basted piece on top of the two layers of batting designated for the left sole. Align the final fabric panel on top of the basted strap panel so that the right sides are facing (the wrong side will be facing up toward you). Pin all four layers together along the outside edge taking care not to catch the center of the strap in the seam allowance. You can fold strap over on itself and pin it at center to keep it a bit flatter.

Beginning at the heel edge, stitch panels together along the outer edge, leaving a 4-in (10-cm) opening at the back (heel). Remove pins, notch curves, and gently turn work right side out by reaching between fabric panels and pulling furthest edge through the heel opening. Press seams.

Insert plastic templates into foot bed between batting layers. Pin opening closed and hand stitch seam shut. Repeat for second slipper.

HELPFUL HINT

Add an edge detail by sandwiching piping or bias tape between the main fabrics along the longer sides of your strap panels. Align the unfinished edges of the trim with the unfinished edges of your fabric. Use a zipper or piping foot which will allow you to stitch very close to the piped edge.

superhero cape and cuffs

Saving the world is quite an undertaking these days. Make sure that your favorite little crusader is properly outfitted for the task at hand with this incredible crime-fighter's cape and a pair of matching cuffs. With a wardrobe like this, the bad guys don't stand a chance.

cape

PREPARATION

Fold fabric in half with right sides facing, so that the folded piece measures 36 in x 22 in (90 cm x 55 cm). Pin layers together around three sides leaving one of the shorter sides open.

ASSEMBLY

Use a ½-in (1.25-cm) seam allowance for this pattern. Stitch along the first side stopping ½ in (1.25 cm) from the end. With needle in the down position, lift presser foot and pivot panel 90 degrees, and continue stitching along second side. Repeat pivot at the next corner and stitch along third side, leaving the final side unstitched. Turn work right side out and press seams.

Stitch along open edge with largest basting stitch, then stitch a second line of basting stitch approximately ¼ in (6 mm) below the first. Gently gather stitching toward center until width is reduced by half, or to desired fullness. Matching unfinished edges, pin the gathered section to the center of the bias tape, and stitch in place along the first fold. Do not trim the bias tape as the additional sections on either side of the panel will be used to tie the cape. Fold bias tape over to enclose the unfinished edge of the cape. Pin in place so that the folds of the bias are aligned, front to back, and topstitch bias closed along its entire length.

cuffs

PREPARATION

The height of my cuffs is 2½ in (6.25 cm) but feel free to alter this measurement if you prefer. Start by measuring the circumference of your child's wrist. To calculate the length of the cuff panel, add 1½ in (3.75 cm) to the wrist width measurement for overlap. The wrist measurement for my cuffs was 6½ in (16.25 cm), so my calculated panel length measurement was 2½ in x 8 in (6.25 cm x 20 cm). Cut two pieces of felt to the size of your calculated measurements.

ASSEMBLY

Wrap cuff panel around wrist and mark inside center of overlap on either side. Stitch Velcro dots to marked positions, so they match when the piece folds over. Consider customizing the cape or cuffs with initials or printed emblems using transfer paper and a tracing wheel.

SAVVY

essential equipment

This section is all about the essential equipment you need to ensure a successful sewing experience. You'll also learn the basics of pattern layout and cutting, commonly used finishing and hand-sewing techniques, proper use and maintenance of sewing equipment, as well as how to troubleshoot common problems.

sewing machines

Get to know your sewing machine intimately by reviewing your manual, where you'll find information about everything from oiling and maintenance to operation and special features.

If you are considering buying a sewing machine, take a little time to research what will be right for you. Visit a reputable dealer for a "test drive," trying out a few new and used brands and models. Use a variety of fabrics during your visit, and make note of the stitch quality and special features of each machine, as well as volume and vibration during use. Many newer machines have wonderful features that are time-savers.

My list of must-haves includes:

High-quality metal chassis and parts: Most cheap machines are built using lots of plastic components that cannot be replaced when they break.

Multiple needle positioning: A must for topstitching, installing zippers, piping, and zigzag stitching.

Adjustable speed: This allows you to slow things down—useful when you are a beginner or when you are trying out new techniques. As you progress, you'll be able to increase speed to knock out projects more quickly.

Droppable feed dogs: Nowadays most machines are equipped with retractable feed dogs. You will want to be sure that you have this option because it allows for multi-directional stitching which is paramount for quilting, darning, and applique, or other decorative curvilinear stitching. Some higher end machines come equipped with other types of multi-directional features, such as monogramming and embroidery functions.

One-step buttonholes: Although buttonholes can be laid out and stitched by hand with almost any sewing machine, a one-step buttonhole feature will allow you to create buttonholes with the press of a button. Some machines also let you program sizing and placement.

Accessories: Check that your sewing machine is equipped with these useful accessories:
- Straight foot—for simple straight stitches.
- Zigzag foot—for zigzags and other decorative stitches.
- Zipper foot—for close stitching with installing zippers.
- Teflon foot—for sewing with sticky fabrics like oilcloth, vinyl, and laminated fabrics.
- Walking foot—for straight-line quilting or when stitching multiple layers of thick fabric through your machine. The dual feed dogs will keep your layers aligned and prevent shifting.
- Free-motion or darning foot—for use with feed dogs dropped for darning holes or quilting curvilinear lines.

cutting tools

Fabric scissors, aka dressmaker's shears: Use your fabric scissors for cutting fabric only. Do not dull or knick the blades by using them on paper or other material. Buy the nicest pair of 7–8 in (17.5–20cm) dressmaking shears you can afford. They should fit your hand comfortably. High-quality brands like Gingher are pricey, but they will last.

Embroidery scissors: You will need a pair of small, delicate embroidery scissors for fine cut work.

Pinking shears: The zigzag cutting edge of pinking shears is a lovely short cut for finishing, helping to prevent fraying, or adding a cute decorative edge to your projects.

Craft scissors: Use craft scissors for cutting paper patterns or anything that isn't fabric.

Rotary cutter and self-healing cutting mat: Rotary cutters are fast and accurate for straight line cutting. Buy the largest blade and mat you can afford to give you more space and allow you to cut through more layers at one time. Never iron on your mat—the heat will warp and ruin it.

Seam ripper: Use a seam ripper to pick out bad stitches, remove erroneous seams, or cut open buttonholes.

pressing tools

Steam iron: A high-quality iron with steam is the key to achieving professional results. Use it to smooth and remove wrinkles from fabric before starting, and to press creases and folds or flatten seams as you work. Be sure to buy a heavy iron that allows you to adjust the amount of steam.

Ironing board: Your ironing board should be well-padded and adjustable to a comfortable height. You should not have to stoop or stretch as you work.

Pressing cloth: A pressing cloth is a piece of protective cloth used when pressing delicate fabrics to prevent scorching, shine, or other marks. A piece of white or unbleached muslin will do just fine if you have that on hand.

measuring and marking tools

Long rulers: Most often made from wood or metal, a yardstick/meter ruler can't be beat for measuring out longer lengths of fabric.

Quilter's square: Designed to be used with rotary cutters, quilter's squares are clear acrylic rulers that are harder wearing than typical sewing rulers. They are more resistant to damage from rotary cutters and have easily readable lines that often include additional angle lines. They are a good investment as their transparency is invaluable for flat measurements, making it easy to check patterns for true "square."

Cloth measuring tape: Essential for taking accurate body measurements, this type of tape measure can stretch out with use, so check it from time to time for accuracy.

Seam gauge: The seam gauge is a tiny ruler for checking seam allowances, marking hems, placing buttonholes, or taking other fine measurements.

Disappearing (or water-soluble) ink markers: Perfect for marking fine lines with precision, but do think about their vanishing properties if you plan to set work aside as your lines may fade before you intend them to. Remember to check for removability in an inconspicuous location on your fabric, and mark on the wrong side when possible.

Tailor's chalk: Tailor's chalk tends to put down a thicker line than marker pens, but you can usually just dust it away on most fabrics. I prefer a basic clay chalk wedge to the waxier versions because they are more easily removable. Buy at least two colors as whatever color you choose will not be visible on a fabric of the same shade. There are a wide variety of pencil and dispensable powder versions too, so experiment to see what works for you. As with all marking tools, check for removability before marking your fabrics. This is especially true when working on the right side of fabrics.

Transfer paper and tracing wheel: These are used in tandem to transfer the lines of a pattern onto fabric or paper. Transfer paper works just like a carbon paper: Place it face down under your pattern, then press firmly along the lines of the pattern with the tracing wheel to imprint markings onto the fabric. Serrated wheels create a dotted line transfer, and smooth wheels make a solid line.

pins

Choose glass-headed pins rather than plastic-headed pins as they are generally of better quality. They are easy to see, to pull from work and pick up when dropped, and best of all, they don't melt when you iron over them.

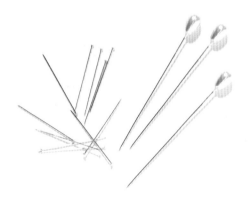

Dressmaker's pins: Ranging in size from 1–1½ in (2.5–3.8 cm), these are great for general use.

Silk pins: Useful for securing delicate fabrics, silk pins have a finer shaft that won't create large holes in your fabric.

Ballpoint pins: Used with jersey fabrics, ballpoint pins have a rounded point that prevents damage to knits.

Appliqué pins: The smallest of all pins, appliqué pins have a length of only ½–¾ in (1.25–1.9 cm).

Quilting pins: Designed for use with lofty or layered fabrics, quilting pins are longer than most other pins at 1½–2 in (3.8–5 cm).

needles

Buy an assortment of sewing needles to start with as it is an inexpensive way to explore your preferences. Sizing for hand-sewing needles is contrary to typical sizing, so the higher the number, the finer the needle. Be sure to use finer needles with thinner fabrics for best results.

Sharps: An all-purpose sewing needle of medium length with a sharp point, sharps are well-suited to closing seams, appliqué work, and hand-piecing.

Betweens: Shorter than sharps, betweens lend themselves to fine, detailed stitching.

Embroidery: Embroidery needles are sharply pointed and have a longer eye to accommodate the thicker, multi-strand threads used for embroidery.

Chenille: Chenille needles have a sharp point for decorative stitching and a large eye that will accommodate ribbons or yarn.

Darners and tapestry: Used for mending, darning holes and needlepoint, darners and tapestry needles are blunt-tipped.

Leather: Heavyweight needles with an unusual triangular, wedge-shaped tip, leather needles are designed for stitching with leather and other heavyweight non-woven fabrics.

sewing machine needles

Using the incorrect needle will inevitably add stress and frustration to your sewing experience. Select sizing appropriate to fabric choices: 70/10 for lightweight and delicate fabrics, 80/12 for medium-weight fabrics, and 90/14 or 100/16 for heavyweight fabrics.

Universal: General purpose needles that work well on most woven fabrics and knits. If you aren't getting good stitch quality consistently, consider switching to a more specialized point.

Stretch: Ballpoint needles appropriate for elastic and elasticized fabric.

Jersey: Ballpoint needles designed to penetrate knits and some stretch materials without damaging fabric.

Jeans or denim: Medium ballpoint needles with a reinforced blade, these can effectively penetrate extra thick fabrics with a reduced risk of skipped stitches and needle breakage.

Leather: Leather needles are heavyweight needles that have a blade point. Do not use these with knits or woven fabrics.

Microtex: Appropriate for silk, microfibers, polyester, and foil fabrics, microtex needles have a slim point.

Metallic: Metallic needles have an elongated eye that creates less friction as thread passes through, so delicate specialty threads shed and break less.

Specialized: Specialized needles include embroidery, topstitch, hemstitch, double-eye, twin, and triple.

thread

For most home sewing projects, all-purpose thread is the right choice. As you progress you may need a wider range of specialty threads, such as elastic thread, machine embroidery, topstitch, or heavyweight upholstery thread. Always choose an appropriate weight, but remember that thread strength should fail before a fabric rips.

This may seem counterintuitive, but you want to be able to repair items along the original seams if they split, and when fabric tears instead of threads breaking, repairs are made more difficult and often impossible.

All-purpose thread: Cotton or polyester, all-purpose thread is the thread you will use most often in your sewing machine and for small hand-sewing jobs. Choose quality brands such as Gutermann or Mettler.

Hand-quilting thread: Consider this for projects where a lot of hand sewing is involved. Hand-quilting thread is slightly heavier in weight than all-purpose thread, so it is less prone to tangles and knotting.

Embroidery thread: Use this for project embellishment and decorative elements. Embroidery thread is commonly made from cotton, linen, silk, and wool. Try stranded and pearl cottons, and crewel and tapestry wools for a variety of looks and textures.

working with fabric

Understanding the characteristics of fabrics will help you to understand how they will perform when used. There are two basic types: wovens and knits. Wovens are fabrics made using a loom to weave together vertical and horizontal threads—fibers that run vertically along the cloth are called warp and fibers that are positioned horizontally are called weft. Knits are created with an industrial knitting machine that uses a series of loops to make fabric from a single thread.

choosing fabric

Every fabric has its own unique qualities based on fiber content and construction. Choose fabrics with drape if you would like a garment that hugs the shape of the body. For a more structured garment, select fabrics with body that will hold their shape. The weight of your fabrics also plays a role, so consider how heavy or light your fabric is and what effect that will have on your overall design. Stretch is added to a wide variety of fabrics; look for high-quality Spandex and Lycra blends to add some spring to your next project.

Cotton and linen: Plant-based fabrics like cotton and linen, which are plainly woven, are some of the easiest to work with because they are neither slippery nor stretchy. As you gain experience and confidence, begin experimenting with other types of fabric to broaden your understanding of fabric characteristics such as weave, drape, and body. Cotton and linen are available in a wide variety of weights, patterns, and textures. Voile, shirting, and handkerchief linens are wonderful choices for lightweight blouses and dresses. Use heavier cottons such as canvas, ticking, corduroy, and denim for pants, skirts, or tote bags.

Silk: Silk is known for its luster, sheen, and drape. This fabric can be very slippery and temperamental, which is why it is often labeled "difficult to sew." However, with a little practice you'll gain the confidence to try sewing with more challenging fabrics. Sample a delicate charmeuse for lingerie, or shiny shantung for a structured jacket.

Wool: Soft and lofty, wool is warm and insulating in winter but breathable in summer. Fabrics made from wool are naturally water and dirt repellent. Try woolen felt for appliqué or small projects that need a lot of body. Flannel, gabardine, and jersey are great for garments.

Non-wovens and laminates: Fabrics like oilcloth, Chalkcloth, Ultrasuede, felt, and leather are part of this grouping, which covers fabrics that cannot be categorized as woven or knit. Man-made or naturally sourced, these materials offer a variety of interesting properties that can be quite useful when properly exploited. Oilcloth, vinyl, and other rubberized materials are wonderfully water repellent. Choose leather, Ultrasuede, or felt for projects that require hard-wearing, stain-resistant materials.

Vintage and recycled fabrics: Using vintage and recycled fabrics adds to the unique qualities of handmade projects. Scour flea markets, antique stores, and the internet for vintage fabrics that are appealing to you, but since shrinking and bleeding colors are more common in vintage fabrics than those currently being manufactured, be sure to prewash.

Batting and stuffing: Batting is a thin, insulating layer that is sandwiched between fabrics for additional warmth and body. High-quality batting does not contain fillers like scrim, binders, or glues. Stuffing is made up of loose fibers that are used to fill toys, cushions, or other three-dimensional pieces. I prefer natural fibers, such as cotton and wool, over synthetics. Wool is lightweight, warm, and lofty. Cotton fiber is washable and has a lovely firmness and density.

Ribbon and trimmings: Use buttons, bias tape, ribbon, rick rack, piping, or pom-poms to add a special detail or an unusual finish.

patterns

Prepare patterns ahead of time. Drafting your own patterns takes a little more time but it allows you to personalize fit and it will help you understand garment construction more fully. Take your time with this part of the process, remembering the adage "measure twice, cut once." Keep in mind that when working from commercial patterns it is usually advisable to work from a slightly larger size and take excess fabric in at the seams.

As with most of the patterns in this book, garments are simply drafted from scratch with little more than a few measurements. Take your time with measurements and follow instructions carefully. Layouts are very basic so don't be overly worried—with a little patience you will be on your way to creating beautiful pieces that are perfectly fitted to you and your home.

Unless otherwise directed, layout pattern pieces so that the fabric grain runs along the center line. Whenever possible, also align grain and cross grain so they are parallel or perpendicular to the straight edges of pattern pieces. Grain (warp thread) runs the length of your fabric parallel to the selvedges (the finished edges on either side of the cloth). Cross grain (weft thread) runs across the fabric at a 90-degree angle to grain.

Be sure to check that the grain of your fabric is square (at a true 90-degree angle) before laying your pattern out. The easiest way to do this is to pull a few threads or tear the fabric across grain near one edge (fig. 1). If it is not "true," realign your edges and smooth the fabric into alignment before laying out pattern pieces. If fabric is especially askew, you can stretch it gently along the bias to straighten warp and weft (fig. 2).

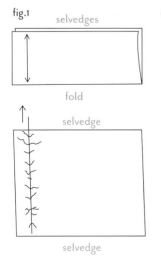

fig.1

selvedges

fold

selvedge

selvedge

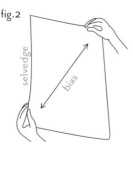

fig.2

selvedge

bias

Once your grain is properly aligned, mark your patterns and fabric with a soft lead pencil, chalk, disappearing ink marker, or transfer paper and tracing wheel. Use whichever transfer method makes the most sense to you, but be sure to test marks in an inconspicuous location to be sure they are removable, and mark on the wrong side whenever possible.

Accurate cutting is also essential to the sewing process. You will want to keep fabric as flat as possible while you are cutting to maintain the integrity of the cut. Take your time and try to keep the bottom edge of your scissors against the tabletop as you work to avoid unnecessary shifting. There are differing opinions about how best to hold your pattern pieces in place while cutting: Some prefer pinning along the pattern edge, some like to trace the outline of pattern pieces directly onto the fabric, and some opt to use pattern weights.

taking measurements

There are three key measurements that you will need to record when sewing garments for yourself: Bust, waist, and hip. Always measure yourself before making up your pattern as in order to create a custom fit you must be absolutely sure of the sizing.

Don't forget to consider the difference between your actual body measurements and the measurements of the finished garment when drafting patterns. This will understandably have a huge impact on how the garment fits.

A form-fitting knit garment should have negative ease, while a form-fitting woven garment will have less ease than a loosely fitting garment. The amount of ease is dependent on the type of fabric (how much stretch it has, if any) and how you want the garment to function.

You can also choose to make a sloper. A sloper, or a basic fitting shell, and it can be a great jumping off point for drafting your own patterns. A library of slopers (a bodice, a pair of pants, a set of sleeves, etc.) will help you create any number of patterns. From the sloper, you'll add length and/or width to various spots to achieve the fit you want.

To measure bust: Place the measuring tape under your arms, wrapping it across the widest part of your back and around the front of your bust at the fullest point.

To measure waist: Your waist measurement should be taken at your natural waistline, which is usually the narrowest part of your body. Bend over and touch your toes; the point where your body folds in half is your waistline.

To measure hip: Be sure to measure around the widest part of your hips.

pressing

While ironing involves a gliding and smoothing of fabric, pressing is a process by which an iron is placed in one area and held, then lifted and placed in another. Use steam to remove stubborn creases, set fabric shape, or press folds and hems. Protect your fabric from scorching and watermarks with a pressing cloth. Always test fabric scraps before applying heat and steam to your project. A tailor's ham and sleeve roll are wonderful tools for pressing curved seams. You can easily make these for yourself with the pattern on page 80.

pinning

Take the time to pin your work and you will be rewarded with excellent results. Pin layers together along the edge with pins at a right angle to that edge. Use your judgment for pin placement and spacing. You will need to use fewer pins for straight cut cottons and more for curves or slippery fabrics. Be sure to pin through fabrics at points that are crucial to alignment.

Never stitch over pins. This results in broken needles and trips to the repair shop. Broken needles also have the potential to cause personal injury. Throw pins—and needles —away if they become bent or dull.

setting up to sew

It is important to set up your sewing machine in an area with good light. Make sure that you are squarely seated in a comfortable chair with both feet on the floor. Maintain good posture and stretch often to avoid neck and back pain. Your machine should be at a reasonable height that eliminates the need to stretch or strain. Pull yourself into your machine: You should be able to reach around and give it a big hug.

Stitching on a machine: Plug your sewing machine into an outlet, and place your foot pedal on the floor so that it is close to your body and you can press on it without stretching. Turn your sewing machine on and follow the instructions for winding a bobbin and threading your machine if this has not yet been done.

Raise your presser foot and slip two layers of fabric under it so the edge of the fabric is aligned to the ½ in (1.25 cm) marking on your throat plate, then lower the presser foot back down—failure to do so will make a mess of your threads when you begin stitching. Next, gently press down on the

foot pedal to engage the motor. Sew a few stitches, then press and hold the reverse button while backstitching to your starting point. Release the reverse and continue to stitch along your seam. Use your left hand to gently guide fabric through the machine, as your right hand directs the edge of your fabric into alignment with the seam allowance guide in front of the needle. Never push or pull your fabric—allow your feed dogs to do the work of moving fabric through the machine. When you reach the end of your stitched line, repeat backstitching. You just sewed your first seam.

Winding a bobbin: Follow the directions in your sewing machine handbook and practice winding a few bobbins. Not all bobbins are alike so be sure to consult your manual to determine which bobbins are appropriate for your machine. Check that bobbins are in good working order before you begin winding. They should be free of nicks, cracks, and warping. Discard any damaged bobbins and replace.

Select a thread appropriate to your project that matches the thread weight and type that you plan to use to thread the top of the machine. Never wind thread over partially full bobbins as this can affect stitch quality. If the thread is not feeding evenly onto your bobbin, check that the thread path is correct and that the thread is untangled. Do not fill bobbin beyond capacity—the added bulk will prevent the bobbin from spinning freely and will cause thread breakage.

Once you have achieved a smooth and even bobbin, load it into your machine as directed in your manual. Pay close attention to threading details to avoid a snarled mess when you start stitching. Be sure to re-engage your handwheel once you have finished winding your bobbins.

Threading the machine: Refer to your manual for proper threading procedures. Select a thread appropriate to your project. Rotate the handwheel toward you until the take-up lever is in its highest position, and lift the presser foot to release pressure from the tension disks.

Place a spool of thread onto the pin at the top right of your machine—the thread should wind off from the back of the spool to the left side of the spool—and follow the charted thread path through the guides on your machine. Pull thread to a length of about 10 in (25 cm) and thread your needle from front to back. Secure the tail of your thread with left hand while rotating the handwheel toward you. Rotate the wheel one full rotation or until the needle drops into the shuttle race and comes back up again. Gently tug the thread in your left hand to pull the lower bobbin thread up through the needle hole. Make sure that both threads are freely moving, and smooth neatly to the left side of your strike plate to prevent threads from becoming tangled.

Changing your needle: Make it a rule to change your needle often. Put in a fresh needle every time you start a new project and replace your needle every few hours. You should also change it if you notice a change in stitch quality, or if it becomes dull and drags while you are sewing. Never use needles that are bent or damaged.

To change your needle, turn the handwheel toward you until your needle is in its highest position. Lower your presser foot to allow for a little more space when accessing the needle clamp (this is the peg or pin extending from the needle bar). Hold the needle with one hand to prevent it from slipping into the opening of the throat plate and gently turn the needle clamp until you can slip the needle from its housing (you may need a micro-screwdriver for this). Insert a fresh needle so that the flat edge is positioned in the slot as the previous needle.

checking tension

Before you begin stitching your project it is a good idea to check your tension and adjust it slightly as needed. Notice that I said "adjust it slightly." Many people actually cause more problems than they solve by making drastic changes to the top tension settings. Over-adjustments can cause unnecessary wear and stress the delicate spring that is responsible for maintaining your top thread tension.

Tension should always be adjusted in very small increments until the perfect balance is achieved. Turning the dial to a higher number will increase the tension of your top thread and turning to a lower number will loosen the tension. Keep in mind most machines stitch a tension suitable for straight stitching on a medium-weight fabric when set to the number 5.

even

loose

tight

Test tension at the start of each project by stitching through a folded scrap of the fabric you plan to use. If you will be using specialty stitches, interfacing, lining, or batting, make sure to use these for your samples so the test is true to the application. You can use contrasting threads for top and bottom to make it easier to see threads on either side of your fabric, but make sure you use threads of the same weight and type.

Balanced tension: Bobbin and spool threads are interlocked within the layers of fabric. Spool thread is only visible on the right side (top) of fabric and bobbin thread is only visible on the wrong side (bottom).

Top tension too loose: Spool thread is visible on the wrong side (bottom) of fabric. Turn tension a half mark higher and sew another line.

Top tension too tight: Bobbin thread is visible on the right side (top) of fabric. Turn the tension a half mark lower to release tension slightly, and stitch another line.

troubleshooting tension

If you have tried adjusting your tension and your issue was not resolved, then check for other common problems:

Rethread your machine: Remove the top thread completely and start from scratch. Double-check the threading diagram in your manual.

Check your bobbin: Remove the bobbin from its case and examine it carefully for damage. Feel for burrs or imperfections and change it out if necessary. Reload bobbin.

Change your needle: If your tension suddenly gets wacky in the middle of a project, change your needle.

techniques and skill builders

This section is designed to help your skill and confidence grow. Use these techniques and skill builders to make sure you can create all of the projects in this book with ease.

backstitch and lock stitch

These techniques secure stitches at the beginning and end of a seam to keep your stitches from unraveling when sewing on a machine. They can usually be used interchangeably, but if less visible results are required choose the lock stitch over the backstitch.

Backstitch: For backstitch, begin your stitch line a few stitches ahead of your desired starting point. Press and hold the reverse button in as you stitch backward for a few stitches, then release the button and continue. When you reach the end, press the button again, and stitch along the seam in reverse for a few stitches.

Lock stitch: For lock stitch, begin sewing with the straight stitch length set to zero. Make a few stitches before resetting stitch length, then continue stitching. Just before you reach the end, reset the stitch length to zero and run a few stitches to lock the seam in place.

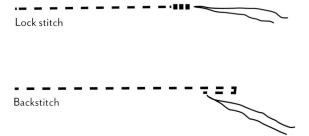

Lock stitch

Backstitch

bias binding

Ribbons cut on the bias (at a 45-degree angle to fabric grain) are called bias binding or bias tape. Available in a variety of widths, pre-folded bias can be purchased in packaged lengths or by the yard/meter, and in single or double fold preparations. As the names suggest, single fold is pre-folded to the center once and double fold is folded over twice (see diagram), and pre-pressed for ease of use. Bias binding can be used to enclose the unfinished edges of a hem, seam, or quilt. It can also be used to make piping, and is ideal for edging and finishing curved seams.

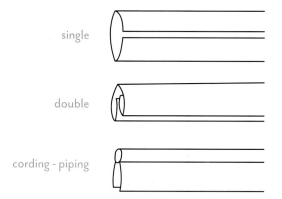

single

double

cording - piping

applying bias binding

Applying bias binding: Unfold your bias binding and pin the wider edge of bias tape into place along the outer edge of the fabric so that the raw edges are aligned. Leave a few inches of bias at either end for fold over. Stitch layers together along pre-pressed fold closest to the edge. Fold unfinished edges over and topstitch into place.

When attaching bias tape to itself, as with enclosed seams like quilt bindings, bias should be stitched together at a 45° angle. To do this leave a few inches of bias unattached at the start and finish of your seam. Where these overlap, fold the top section of tape at a 45° angle and crease it firmly with your fingers. Next, mark the bias tape below it along that fold. Now fold your tape out and situate the ends of bias tape with right sides facing at a 90 degree angle (they should be crossing one another like an X). Pin and stitch together so that the 45° line that you just drew aligns with the crease you made. Trim excess fabric and stitch along fold to finish. Fold over as above to enclose edges.

make your own bias binding

Perfectly coordinated patterns in any width are knocked out in a flash with this short-cut continuous bias method. I usually use ½–¾ yd (½–¾ m) medium-weight cotton to make a whole heap of tape, and a bias tape maker to speed the process even further.

Start by folding fabric in half so right sides are facing, and stitch open edges together (A). Draw a line diagonally across your fabric and trim the corners connected by this line. Insert your scissors into one of the snipped corners and cut top layer of fabric along the line (B). Turn panel over and draw another diagonal line between the two remaining uncut corners (C). Trim corners away and cut through upper layer along this second line. If you cut everything just right, your panel should unfold into a tube.

Lay your tube on a flat surface. Measure and mark a line at least 6 in (15 cm) from—and parallel to—the fold in your tube (D). Measure and mark lines spaced to the width of your bias tape perpendicular to the parallel line drawn (E). (If you are using a bias tape maker, consult the measurement requirements on the packaging.) Cut along marked edges to the parallel line: Do not cut beyond this point. Open the uncut section of the fabric and smooth loops out of the way. Trim work diagonally across the uncut section to create a single spiraling piece of fabric. Cut from the bottom right corner to the first line on the left, then from the first line on the right to the second on the left, and so on (F). Trim away any uneven segments at the beginning and end of your bias so that the tape is even. Fold fabric over cording and use your zipper foot to seam in place, or use directions on your bias tape maker to create a single fold or double fold bias tape.

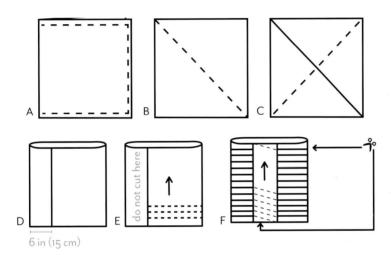

6 in (15 cm)

notching, clipping and curves

Concave curves (A): Trim edge to half the original width and cut into seam allowance to about ⅛ in (3 mm) from stitches, to allow seam to stretch out and lay flat inside the seam.

Convex curves (B): Cut a series of triangular notches to about ⅛ in (3 mm) from stitching, to allow the seam to compress without creating unsightly lumps or overlaps.

Corners (C—inward facing): Clip into the seam allowance toward your pivot point, stopping ⅛ in (3 mm) from stitches.

Corners (D—outward facing): Trim away the corner of your fabric about ⅛ in (3 mm) above the pivot point and remove the small triangular section of fabric. Trim additional bulk as needed, taking care to leave seam intact with at least ⅛-in (3-mm) seam allowance.

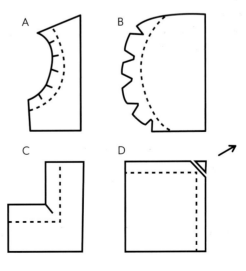

buttons and buttonholes

If your machine doesn't have an automatic one-step buttonhole feature, you will need to layout and stitch them manually. First, calculate your buttonhole sizing by measuring the width of the button, add to that the height of the button, and another ⅛ in (3 mm) for a bit of ease. Once you know the size of your buttonholes, mark them out on your fabric with even spacing. Mark the centerline of the buttonhole, as well as the start and end points—your mark should resemble a capital "H" on its side.

Most machines have programmed manual buttonhole settings, so you will want to consult your manual for the specifics of your model. If yours does not, you can make a lovely reinforced buttonhole using machine zigzag stitch. Begin by setting the width of your zigzag to a shorter length and width. Stitch along the left side of the marked centerline to the bottom, ending with your needle in the down position at left. Pivot your work 180 degrees and stitch along the other side of the marked line back to your start point (A). Reset your stitch width so that it spans both rows of stitches and dial the stitch length to just above zero. Sew a few wide stitches to finish one end of your buttonhole, ending with your needle in the down position (B). Make a note of the stitch settings you used so that you can replicate them at the other end of your buttonhole. Pivot your work, lower your presser foot and raise your needle. Reset your machine to straight stitching and sew along the inside of one of your zigzags to the other end (C). With your needle raised, reset your zigzag stitch settings as noted and stitch the other end of your buttonhole to finish (D). Use your seam ripper to cut the buttonhole open along the centerline, taking great care to avoid cutting into your stitches.

Lay fabric out so that buttonholes overlap closure point with desired alignment and place a pin through the center of each buttonhole to mark button placement on the other side. Securely stitch buttons into place at the marked points.

Sewing a button: There are two types of buttons—shank and sew through. Shank buttons have a small protrusion at the back of the button and are used for heavyweight applications such as jackets and winter coats. Sew through buttons usually have two or four holes in the center and are used commonly for dress shirts and other lighter weight clothing.

Shank buttons: Push a threaded needle through fabric from back to front at the marked point. Pass the needle through the shank of the button and return it to the wrong side through your original entry point. Pull thread tight, drawing the button shank to the fabric. Repeat these steps, looping the needle and thread through the fabric and shank alternately several times, until button is securely fastened. Bring needle to the wrong side of your work, make a knot in the thread close to the exit point, and pass through the stitches on the back of the work to secure tail. Trim excess thread.

Sew through buttons: Mark the location of each hole in your button. Bring threaded needle up through fabric from the wrong side of the work at the first marked point. Pass your needle through the first hole in your button, from back to front. Insert your needle into the second hole and draw your thread back through the fabric at the second marked point to the wrong side. Place a thick darning needle under your button between your stitches, and pull the button tight to your fabric. Repeat to alternately loop your needle and thread through the holes in your button several times, until your button is firmly attached to your fabric.

Now, bring your needle to the front of the fabric but do not loop your thread through the button. Instead, wrap your thread around the looped threads under the button several times and pull your thread tight. Remove the darning needle and wrap a few more times before passing the needle to the back of the work. Tie a knot close to your fabric. Pass thread through the stitches at the back of the work to secure tail, and trim excess thread.

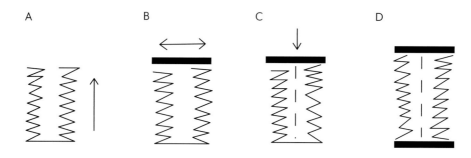

double fold hem

Finish edges in a tidy manner by enclosing them in the fold of a double fold hem. Using a ruler or seam gauge, fold the fabric edge over to the desired width and press along fold (A). Fold fabric over a second time and pin folded edge into place at the desired width (B). Edge-stitch seam and press hem to finish (C).

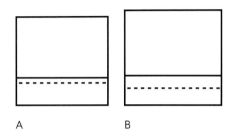

A   B   C

edge stitch and topstitch

Straight stitching is used in both of these techniques to finish, reinforce, or add decoration to projects. Edge-stitching is a visible seam sewn very close to the edge—⅛ in (3 mm) or less (A). Topstitching is very similar to edge-stitching but it is stitched a bit farther in from the edge (B) at about ¼ in (6 mm). In both cases the stitches are parallel to the seam.

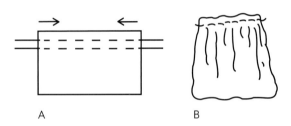

A   B

gathering and ruffles

This technique is an easy way to add interesting detail and volume to projects. Cut fabric 1½–2 times the desired length of your ruffle. Set your sewing machine to the longest straight stitch length, baste two parallel lines along the edge to be gathered. Now gently pull your bobbin (bottom) thread and gather your fabric evenly from either side toward the center of the work (A). When fabric is condensed to desired measurement, stitch along the gathered edge, making sure to backstitch at each end to secure the ruffle, and remove basting stitches (B).

A   B

zigzag

This zigzag stitch is a versatile machine stitch for finishing edges, and its stretchy properties makes it an ideal choice for seaming knits, jersey, and stretch fabrics. You will need to adjust the stitch width on your machine to create this saw-toothed stitch, and be sure to use a needle appropriate to your fabric choice.

finishing seams

Consider finishing your seams to add strength, tame bulk, prevent fraying, or add visual appeal.

Clean seam: Use the clean seam method if your sewing machine does not zigzag. Press seam open and stitch ⅛–¼ in (3–6 mm) from the raw edges on each side.

Pinked seam: For fabric that is not prone to fraying, use pinking shears to trim excess fabric along the edge of the seam, then press the pinked seam open.

Zigzag seam: This finish is achieved by applying a zigzag along the raw edge of your seam allowance. This can be used to enclose rough edges and combat fraying on almost any type of seam. Sew a zigzag stitch along the unfinished edge of your seam allowance so that one side of your stitch just misses over the edge of your fabric. If you are pressing seams to one side, treat your seam allowances as one piece. If you are pressing seams open, stitch each edge separately. Press seams again after applying zigzag to help fabric fiber relax.

French seams: French seams offer a more refined finish than the pinked and zigzag seam finishing as cut edges are enclosed inside the seam. Remember to take into account the additional fold over when you are calculating your measurements for seam allowance. Starting with wrong sides facing, sew a seam ¼ in (6 mm) from the edge of your fabric (A). Trim seam allowance to ⅛ in (3 mm). Fold fabric so right sides are facing, press seam, and pin layers together (B). Stitch another seam ¼ in (6 mm) from the first seam. Open seam out and press seam allowance to one side (C).

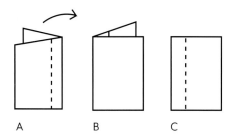

A   B   C

Bias tape: Bias tape can also be used to finish seams and add a special detail where bulk is not an issue. Fold bias tape open, align wider unfinished edge of bias to the unfinished edge of your seam; pin together. Stitch a seam on the pre-pressed crease, then fold tape over to enclose raw edges. To ensure proper stitching, pin through the layers to make sure folds are matched on either side, and topstitch bias into place. See pages 108–109 for further information.

mitered corners

A mitered corner (sometimes called a mitered hem) is a seaming technique that allows for a very flat finish on cornered seams, perfect for window treatments, tea towels, quilt binding, and detailing on garments.

Begin by turning and pressing a double fold hem on two adjacent sides of a square panel—hems will overlap at the corner. Unfold hems to see pressed lines; the point where your pressed lines intersect is the starting point for your seam (see A). Fold fabric in half diagonally from the corner where your seams meet, so the fabric forms a triangle. Pin through your layers so edges are carefully aligned and mark a line at a 45-degree angle from the pivot point—the inner pressed line at the fold where your seams meet—to the outer fold line (B). Now stitch along the line you just marked using a lock stitch at beginning and end points to secure stitching. Cut excess fabric at corner, trimming a little near the tip if needed (C). Press seam open and turn work right side out along previously pressed hem lines (D). Fold unfinished edge under and edge-stitch along fold (E).

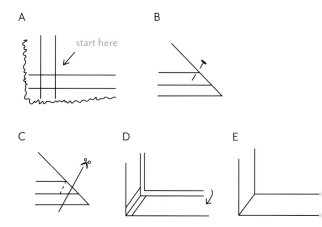

A   B

start here

C   D   E

pivoting

Accurately stitch pointed corners using pivoting. This adds strength to your corners because there are no breaks in the thread that can weaken over time. Stitch your seam as usual, and when you reach the starting point of the next seam—a seam allowance width from the edge—end with your needle in the down position (A). Lift presser foot and turn your work 90 degrees, lower presser foot, and continue stitching.

A

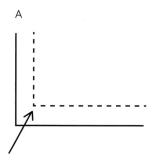

pom-poms

Create these fun little fluff balls by wrapping yarn around your thumb and index finger in a figure-of-eight fashion (A). When your wrapping is nice and thick, slip loops off, and tie bundle around the center securely. Use your scissors to cut through loops (B). Fluff the fibers of your pom-pom, and trim to adjust smoothness and shape if necessary.

A   B

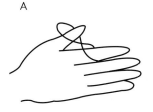

zippers

To install a centered zipper, mark the position of your zipper along the seam with pins at each end point. Secure the ends of the seam with a few backstitches at the marked points on either side, and baste the seam together between the pins (A). Finish the edges of your seam with pinking shears or a zigzag stitch, and press seam open (B). With right side facing down, position your zipper so that the teeth are aligned over the basted section with the ends overlapping the backstitches at each end (C). Baste zipper into place and turn work to right side. Mark out the stitch line (usually about ¼ in/6 mm) on either side of the basted seam and at each end of zipper (D). Be careful not to mark over the stopper or pull; stitching over these will break your needle. Attach your zipper foot and stitch along the marked line, pivoting at each corner (E). Remove basting stitches and test your zipper.

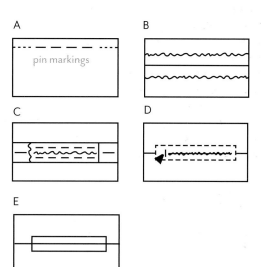

hand stitching and embroidery

Although decorative stitches and fancy seams are not absolutely necessary, learning these hand stitches and embroidery techniques will make your sewing projects extra special.

double looped knot

A sturdy, well-formed knot, useful when you need something a bit heavier. Make a loop in your thread and pass one end through the loop (A). Bring the end around to the back and slip it through the loop again (B). Pull thread at both ends to tighten knot (C).

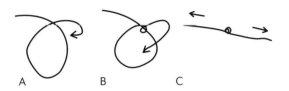

basting

Basting stitches are long, loose, running (straight) stitches, often done by hand for easy removal. They can be used to temporarily join fabrics, hold layers of fabric together, and to manage unruly or slippery fabrics. I like to use a contrasting thread to make stitches visible, and you should always be sure to baste to one side of the line you intend to sew so that you don't weaken or damage your stitches when removing the basting stitches. When using your machine to baste, set the stitch length to the longest setting for best results.

running stitch (aka straight stitch)

The most basic hand sewing stitch. You can use it for attaching trims, basting, or as a decorative stitch.

Working from right to left, use a rocking motion to move the needle in and out of the fabric several times before you pull the needle and thread through to tighten your stitch line. Practice evenly measured and spaced stitches. For securing trims and permanent seams, make your stitches as small as possible; work longer stitches for basting.

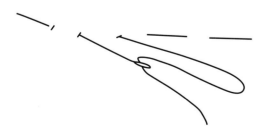

whip stitch (aka overcast stitch)

Use whip stitch for hemming, joining finished edges, applying layers, and embroidery.

Insert your needle into the hem or applied edge, and draw needle and thread toward you. Inserting your needle into main fabric perpendicular to the seam, pick up a thread or two of each fabric along the edge of the seam where they meet. Pull the needle toward you and repeat. Work evenly across the fabric with small stitches about ⅛ in (3 mm) apart for finer work.

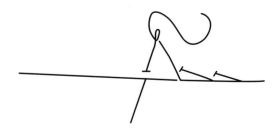

blind stitch (aka slip stitch or invisible stitch)

This hand sewing stitch is the most invisible of all stitches. It is great for hemming, appliqué elements, and attaching trim or binding along the edge of a fabric.

Pick up a stitch in the hem or folded edge then pick up a small stitch in the main fabric just across from the exit point of the first stitch. Pick up another stitch in the fold and continue in this manner, working back and forth along the seam you are securing. Gently pull your thread and the stitches will disappear into the seam.

backstitch

Increase your stitch strength when hand sewing seams, or add this versatile stitch to your embroidery repertoire for a weightier decorative line. This stitch is especially suited to angular lines that require a crisper, clean edge.

Make a stitch by drawing your needle up through the fabric and back down into it. Bring your needle back up through the fabric a stitch length ahead of the stitch you just made. Insert your needle into the fabric through the hole at the end of your last stitch and pull to thread to the back side of your work. Repeat.

chain stitch

One of my favorite decorative stitches, chain stitch adds texture and delicate intricacy to any line or shading application.

Bring needle through fabric and pull thread to the front of the work. Reinsert needle into your exit hole and pull thread until a small loop remains at the top of the work, bringing your needle back through the front of the fabric to catch the loop at center. Gently pull thread to secure stitch against fabric. Repeat to end.

french knot

This decorative darling has an undeserved reputation for being difficult. Follow these simple steps and you'll embroider these delicate dots with authority.

Bring needle thread through your fabric and pull thread through to the front. With your non-dominant hand, hold the thread taut a few inches from where it exits the fabric. Place your needle in front of and perpendicular to the thread and wind thread over the needle twice (A). Maintaining tension, reinsert needle into your fabric just next to your original exit point (B). Stabilizing your wraps against the fabric, push the needle through the fabric, and pull thread to the wrong side.

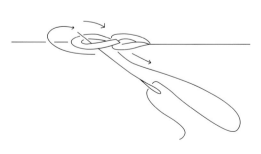

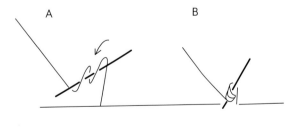

templates

crown of flowers *page 15*
template shown at actual size

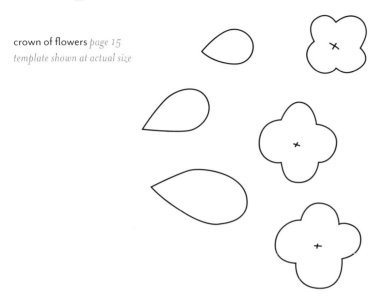

stuffed owls *page 39*
template shown at actual size

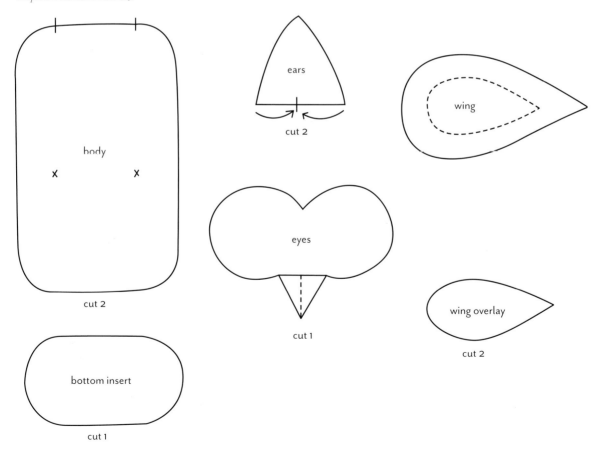

juggling balls *page 41*
template shown at actual size

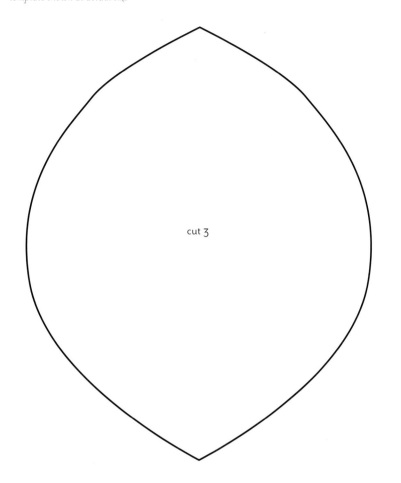

cut 3

eye mask *page 52*
increase template by 50%

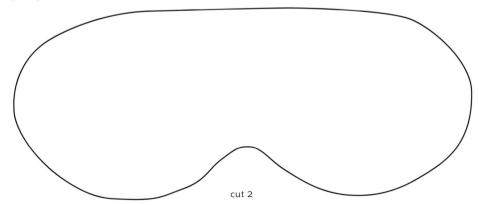

cut 2

pincushion *page 54*
increase template by 50%

glasses case *page 56*
increase template by 50%

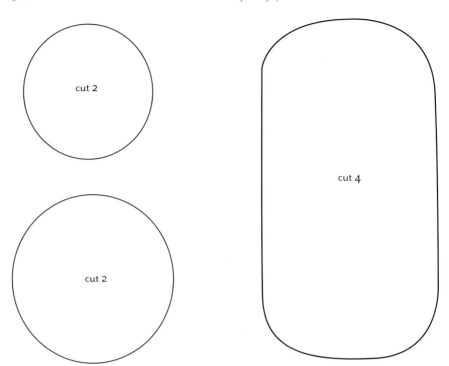

cut 2

cut 2

cut 4

hand warmers *page 66*
template shown at actual size

cut 2

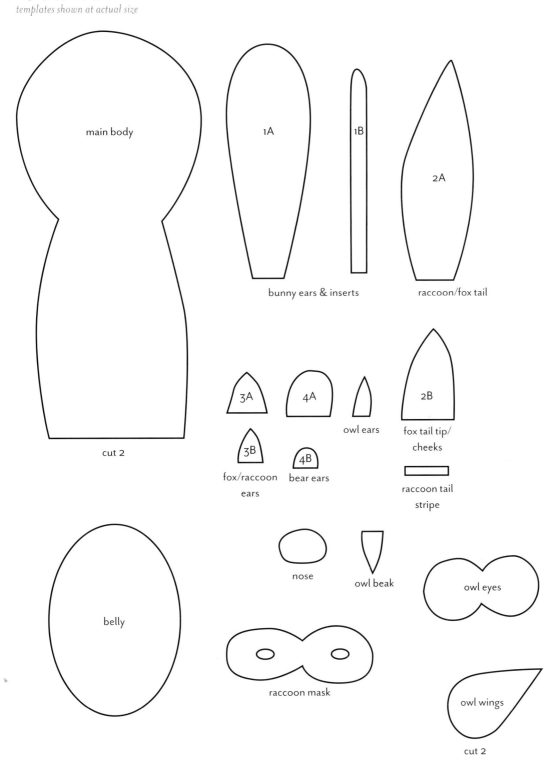

main body

cut 2

1A

1B

bunny ears & inserts

2A

raccoon/fox tail

3A

4A

owl ears

2B

fox tail tip/
cheeks

3B

fox/raccoon
ears

4B

bear ears

raccoon tail
stripe

belly

nose

owl beak

owl eyes

raccoon mask

owl wings

cut 2

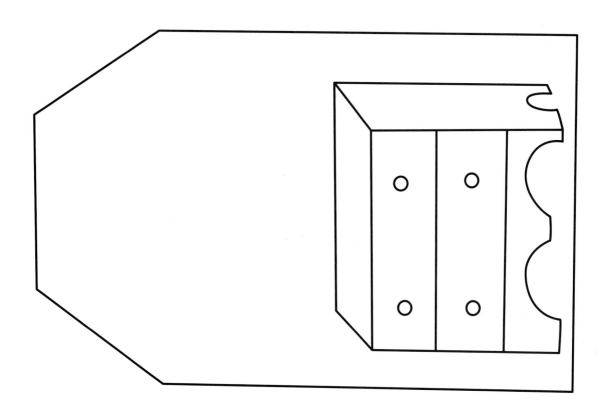

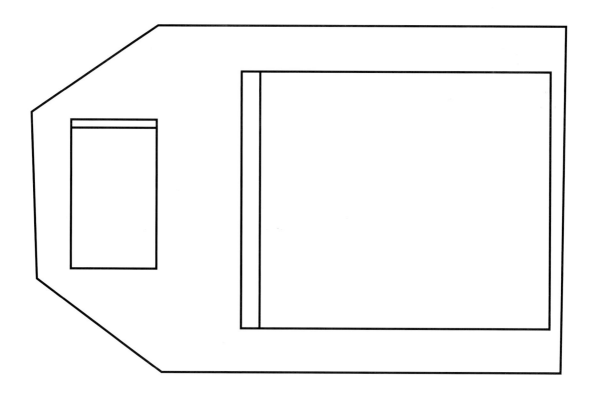

flat doll dress up *page 70*
increase templates by 50%

stuffed bunny *page 72*
increase templates by 50%

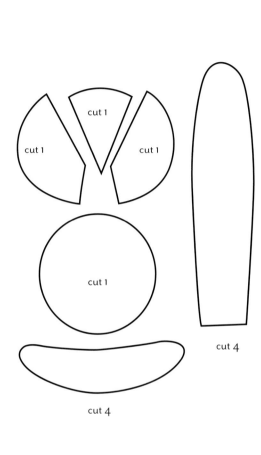

cut 1

cut 1

cut 1

cut 1

cut 4

cut 4

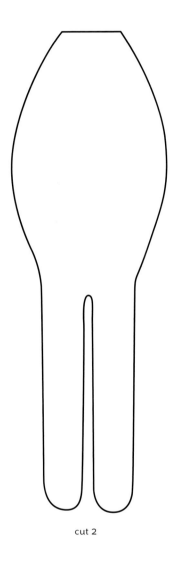

cut 2

robot rattle *page 74*
template shown at actual size

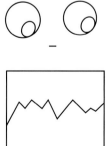

paper plane mobile *page 76*
template shown at actual size

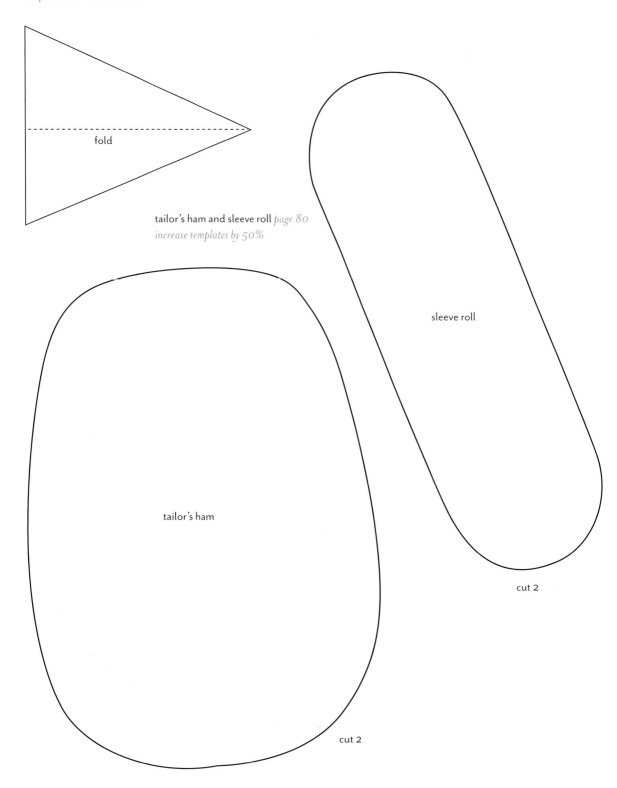

fold

tailor's ham and sleeve roll *page 80*
increase templates by 50%

sleeve roll

tailor's ham

cut 2

cut 2

change purse *page 81*
template shown at actual size

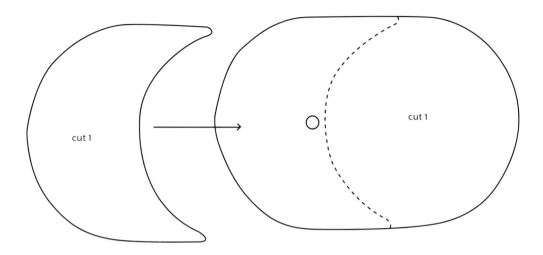

cut 1

cut 1

bike basket *page 87*
increase templates by 50%

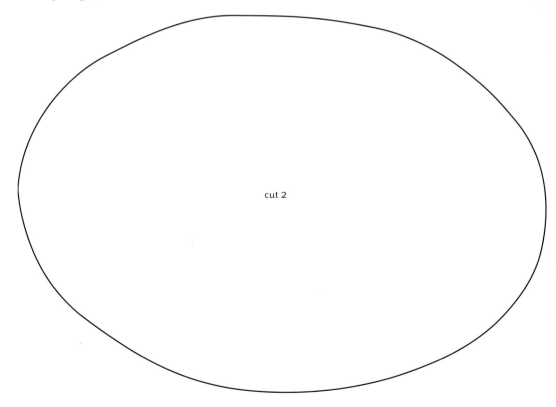

cut 2

index

Page numbers in **bold** type refer to templates; numbers in *italic type* refer to photographs.

acknowledgments

Thank you to everyone who helped to make this wonderful book a reality. For my mother, thank you for teaching me to sew and other life lessons. To my partner, Kevin Hopper, thank you for your love and patience—life with you is an amazing adventure. A special thank you to my lovely, creative friends Larra Nebel, Kate Fraher and Nguyen Le—your kindness, generosity and wisdom are unmatched. Mark Searle, Caroline Elliker, Cheryl Brown and everyone at Quintet, thank you so much for your guidance and support throughout this process.

MANUFACTURERS

Alexander Henry Fabrics is a registered trademark of Alexander Henry Fabrics, Inc. Art Gallery Fabrics is a registered trademark of Art Gallery Quilts, LLC. Benartex is a registered trademark of Benartex. LLC. Birch Fabrics is a registered trademark of Birch Fabrics. Cloud9 Fabrics is a registered trademark of Cloud9 Fabrics, Inc. Schumacher is a registered trademark of F. Schumacher & Co. Free Spirit Fabric is a registered trademark of Westminster Fibers, Inc. KOKKA is a registered trademark of KOKKA Co., Ltd. LECIEN is a registered corporation of LECIEN Corporation. Liberty of London is a registered trademark of Liberty, Ltd. Marcus Fabrics is a registered trademark of MARCUS BROTHERS TEXTILES, INC. Michael Miller Fabrics is a registered trademark of Michael Miller Fabrics. Moda Fabrics is a registered trademark of United Notions. Monaluna is a registered trademark of Monaluna. Oilcloth is a registered trademark of Oilcloth International, Inc. Red Rooster Fabrics is a registered trademark of Red Rooster Fabrics. Robert Kaufman Fabrics is a registered trademark of Robert Kaufman Co. Rowan is a registered trademark of Westminster Fibers, Inc. Waverly Fabrics is a registered trademark of Iconix Brand Group, Inc. Windham Fabrics is a registered trademark of Windham Fabrics. All other trademarks are the property of their respective owners none of whom are affiliated to or endorse this book.

SUPPLIERS

B&J Fabrics, Bernina International AG, Brooklyn General Store, City Quilter, Fiber Notion, hellomello *handspun*, Hyman Hendler & Sons, Keepsake Quilting, M&J Trimming, Make Workshop, Mood Fabrics, Pacific Trimming, Purl Soho, Tender Buttons, Textile Arts Center.

QUINTET PUBLISHING WOULD ALSO LIKE TO THANK

Don Speake & Company Ltd, Focus Photographic Locations and Nathalie Fell of Needham's Models.